BACKGROUND
KNOWLEDGE

BACKGROUND KNOWLEDGE

the missing piece of
the comprehension
puzzle

DOUGLAS FISHER
NANCY FREY

HEINEMANN
Portsmouth, NH

Heinemann
361 Hanover Street
Portsmouth, NH 03801–3912
www.heinemann.com

Offices and agents throughout the world

The authors and publisher wish to thank those who have generously given permission to reprint borrowed material:

Cartoon "Evolution of Communication" by Mike Keefe from *The Denver Post* and InToon.com, March 27, 2009. Reproduced by permission of dePIXion Studios, Inc.

"Where I'm From" by George Ella Lyon from *Where I'm From: Where Poems Come From* by George Ella Lyon. Copyright © 1999 by George Ella Lyon. Published by Absey & Co., Inc. Reproduced by permission of the author.

(*credits continue on page 191*)

Library of Congress Cataloging-in-Publication Data
Fisher, Douglas.
  Background knowledge : the missing piece of the comprehension puzzle / Douglas Fisher and Nancy Frey.
     p. cm.
  Includes bibliographical references and index.
  ISBN-13: 978-0-325-02655-8
  ISBN-10: 0-325-02655-6
  1. Reading comprehension—Study and teaching (Middle school). 2. Reading comprehension—Study and teaching (Secondary). 3. Content area reading.
I. Frey, Nancy.   II. Title.

LB1573.7.F55 2009
428.4071'2—dc22   2009016165

Editor: Wendy Murray
Production editor: Lynne Costa
Cover design: Shawn Girsberger
Typesetter: House of Equations, Inc.
Manufacturing: Valerie Cooper

Printed in the United States of America on acid-free paper
13   12   11   10   09   VP   1   2   3   4   5

Contents

Foreword

In your hands is an important new book, *Background Knowledge*. This is a highly engaging, informative, and imminently practical conversation with two of the leading scholars in secondary reading comprehension and school learning. Doug Fisher and Nancy Frey have taken on the challenge of our times: How do we prepare *all* students for the reading comprehension and learning demands they will face every day—in school and throughout their adult lives? They answer this question in powerful ways throughout this new and important contribution to our understanding of effective instruction in subject area classes.

Improving the ability to read, comprehend, and learn is one of our most pressing educational priorities. Despite extensive effort, many students continue to struggle, increasing the possibility they will drop out of school. It is essential that all students become fully prepared in reading comprehension so that each and every individual succeeds in school, fulfills individual goals, and makes our world a better place through his or her accomplishments. Doug and Nancy show us how.

Grounded in the central research studies and national reports on literacy and learning, their book adds an important new dimension to our understanding of classroom instruction. The special focus of this book is on developing background knowledge through classroom instruction, a central aspect of reading comprehension and learning in every subject area classroom.

If you work with students in grades 6–12, the book that you hold in your hands is a special treasure. Doug and Nancy will show you the role of background knowledge in reading comprehension and learning. You will also discover how to systematically develop this essential aspect of reading comprehension, preparing students in all subject areas for their learning and literacy future.

There are several distinctive features to this volume. Most strikingly, the writing is clear, compelling, and personable. You will come to know both Doug and Nancy as your guides on this journey. They understand your classroom experiences and they share theirs. They provide an abundance of highly practical instructional ideas, designed to increase background knowledge and improve the comprehension of content area information. Each instructional practice is closely connected to central conclusions from the research literature, always in a manner that can be put to immediate use in your classroom. This is a book written by authors who know the classroom in all its complexity, diversity, and richness. Doug and Nancy teach; they do not simply talk.

We know that each subject area has its own special requirements. Doug and Nancy connect these requirements to comprehension instruction, with examples from each of the major subject areas. They also include a separate chapter on the new literacies of online reading comprehension, showing the many new skills required for effective reading comprehension and learning with information on the Internet.

Finally, this book is wonderfully cohesive and well organized. You will find the model of instruction, presented in Chapter 2, familiar and easy to use. Doug and Nancy apply this model to the development of background knowledge in a progressive, increasingly rich fashion. I appreciated the time these authors took to carefully structure the presentation of information. I know you will as well.

During the recent past, we have not paid adequate attention to the essential role of background knowledge in reading comprehension and learning. Doug Fisher and Nancy Frey return us to this powerful insight. Can we actually teach background knowledge and improve learning opportunities for all students in powerful ways? As Doug and Nancy remind us, "Yes, we can!"

—Donald J. Leu
Director, The New Literacies Research Lab
John and Maria Neag Endowed Chair in Literacy and Technology
University of Connecticut

The Missing Piece of the Comprehension Puzzle

BACKGROUND KNOWLEDGE. MIGHT IT RESCUE the next generation of readers? That might be melodramatic, but we do think that our middle and high school students are in danger. They're at risk because there has been such an intense focus on improving reading comprehension and getting children reading for standardized tests that teachers' attention to considering students' background knowledge has waned. There are many complex reasons some of our secondary students are not where they should be as readers. In this book we want to put forth the idea that one reason is an overemphasis in the field on comprehension strategy instruction. Of course strategy instruction is important, but it's not sufficient. We need to look at classrooms nationwide and assess how strategies are being taught, help teachers teach them effectively, and stress that they are one of several aspects of learning to read.

Consider the following sentence from a neuroanatomy text:

> Improved vascular definition in radiographs of the arterial phase or of the venous phase can be procured by a process of subtraction whereby positive and negative images of the overlying skull are superimposed on one another.

Which comprehension strategy will help you make meaning from this text? Can you predict? Infer? How about summarize? None of the words are that hard—you probably know what an image is and how to subtract. The overall difficulty of the text is within your reading range. Certainly you have the decoding ability necessary to read this sentence and you can probably read it with reasonable fluency. Why is it, then, that this is so hard to understand? By now, you're probably saying to yourself, "I don't have the background knowledge to really understand this." Yes, exactly.

How much a reader already knows about the subject is probably the best predictor of reading comprehension. When readers engage with a text for which they have limited background knowledge, the text is much more difficult to understand than one for which they have ample background knowledge. So while the reading world is focused on leveling books and comprehension strategy instruction, research indicates that children continue to spin their wheels when they don't have the background knowledge required to understand much of what they are reading (Fisher, Frey, and Lapp 2009; Langer 1984).

In order for background knowledge to be useful, a learner must be able to locate it and then apply it. This sounds straightforward, but this statement masks the complexities that have vexed teachers (and parents) throughout time. A teenager's closet is a good analogy here. We've all had experiences with sending an adolescent to his room to retrieve an item, say a backpack. Now, you know the teen owns a backpack; you paid for it yourself. But whether that teenager can locate it is another matter altogether. The problem may be that the closet, which holds the backpack, is completely disorganized. On the other hand, the issue may not be organization, but rather knowing when the backpack is needed. Further, there may be an issue of motivation; perhaps the teenager doesn't yet care whether or not he has his school stuff with him.

Have you found yourself reminding that adolescent every school day that he needs to get his backpack before leaving the house? He knows where it is, but for some reason isn't conditioned to *when* he will need it. It's also possible that he shows the same tendencies at school—he leaves his belongings behind in classrooms and rarely arrives at a new activity with the tools he needs to complete the task. In this case, he's not transferring from one situation to the next, especially when they are new activities. The inability to use one or more of these factors—knowing where to find something, knowing when you need it, knowing how to use it in a new situation, or wanting to have it available—interferes with performance. In other words, possession alone isn't enough.

The National Research Council's report *How People Learn: Brain, Mind, Experience, and School* describes a framework for understanding how background knowledge supports new learning:

> The new science of learning does not deny that facts are important for thinking and problem solving. . . . However, the research also shows clearly that "usable knowledge" is not the same as a mere list of disconnected facts. Experts' knowledge is connected and organized around important concepts (e.g., Newton's second law of motion); it is "conditionalized" to specify the contexts in which it is applicable; it supports understanding and transfer (to other contexts) rather than only the ability to remember. (2000, 11)

Let's take these three concepts—that knowledge must be organized, conditionalized, and transferable—and look more closely at the evidence for each.

■ Organized

Schema theory lies at the heart of organization, the first provision necessary for background knowledge to be useful (McVee, Dunsmore, and Gavelek 2005). A schema represents a hierarchical representation of knowledge, connected to other related information. For example, your knowledge of pizza includes its characteristics (food, round, dough, red sauce), types of pizza (cheese, vegetarian, pepperoni), and pizzas that don't fit all the usual characteristics (square pan, BBQ chicken). In addition, your schema for pizza is connected to other schemata (food, sports events, restaurants, Italy). Rumelhart (1984) described the characteristics of schemata as representative of knowledge (rather than isolated facts), nested within other schemata, variable, and acted upon by the learner. Aspects of schema theory are embedded in the learning theories forwarded by Piaget, Rosenblatt, and Dewey (McVee, Dunsmore, and Gavelek 2005).

We were provided an interesting way of thinking about schemata by one of the reviewers of this book, who explained it like this: Throw a handful of paper clips on the table. They scatter into a random mess, much like the bits of knowledge in some students' heads. But if you use a large magnet, the individual pieces will gather together and connect to something bigger. And that is a schema.

You can easily retrieve your useable knowledge of pizza because it is organized and connected to other facts. An important factor in your ability to maintain this organizational structure is the fact that it is clustered around a big idea rather than simply a bunch of isolated facts. In contrast, consider a topic that may not be well organized in your mind—it may be opera, or car engines, or rugby. In any of these cases, if you are not an expert or have not developed an organizational structure, you might be able to come up with a few facts (*Carmen* is an opera, or it's not over until the fat lady sings) and you might be able to link them (operas, like car engines and rugby, are noisy), but that's about it. Unfortunately, this isn't good for learning.

However, a learner who possesses a schema for knowledge can draw upon it in much more sophisticated ways. You may have a great deal of knowledge about operas, or car engines, or rugby, which is influenced by your prior experiences and your interest. These prior experiences include those that occurred both inside and outside the classroom. Therefore, teachers who organize new knowledge in ways that support the development of schemata are making it possible for learners to find it in their mental closets when they need it again. The National Research Council notes, "Expert teachers know the structure of their disciplines, and this knowledge provides them with cognitive roadmaps that guide the assignments they give students, the assessments they use to gauge students' progress, and the questions they ask in the give and take of classroom life. In short, their knowledge of the discipline and their knowledge of pedagogy interact" (2000, 155).

Experience with learning plays a role as well. As adolescents engage with more formal disciplines during the middle and high school years, they are required to assimilate knowledge into increasingly more complex schemata. Here again, the teacher is an important part of this equation. Students can benefit from organizational aids such as note taking and graphic organizers precisely because the tools mirror the mental models they should be constructing (Robinson 1998; Williams and Eggert 2002).

For example, during a unit of study on plants, tenth grader Ashley was able to activate her background knowledge about cellular structure to understand the similarities and differences between plant and animal cells. She also had an organizational schema for living things and was able to use that knowledge and apply it to plants. She described, "All living things must be capable of homeostasis, organization, metabolism, growth, adaptation, response to stimuli, and reproduction. I'm organizing my notes by these seven factors because I know that they all have to be present because plants are living things."

■ Conditionalized

The second factor necessary for background knowledge to be useable is conditionalism; that is, the learner must know where and when to apply it. Remember the scenario of the teenager who knows where his backpack is but never seems to remember to get it when preparing to leave the house for school? That's someone who is not yet conditionalized. And yes, part of conditionalized learning relates to motivation. If a person is motivated, he is more likely to apply what he knows almost automatically. That said, we're not speaking so much of behavioral conditioning as we are of the decision making that goes on in a learner's head as he determines what background knowledge he should apply. Rumelhart (1984) characterized schemata as being nested within other schemata, an argument in support of the practice of fostering connections across knowledge bases and disciplines.

We were reminded of this while observing a ninth-grade English teacher friend of ours during a think-aloud based on the short story *Kipling and I*, by Jesus Colon. As part of her think-aloud, she identified relevant background knowledge and noted why this was important. She told the students,

> I don't know why he has to read by the light from the street lamp. Oh, but now I remember the pictures I found of New York at the turn of the century. Lots of people didn't have electricity. They thought life would be better by immigrating to the U.S., but it wasn't. They were poor and often couldn't afford electricity. So now this makes sense; he's reading by the streetlight because he doesn't have his own light in his apartment!

With that one think-aloud, the teacher demonstrated how her brain clicked through related schemata to call forth the information that she needed to understand a text's detail.

Another useful image to consider is that while all the background knowledge of the world is vast—a mess of paper clips—it's an ordered universe when you look at it arranged into disciplines. And within these disciplines, there are hierarchies of information and concepts. Consider, for example, the stance held by some science educators that physics should precede biology and chemistry (Bardeen and Lederman 1998). They assert that physics principles govern other scientific concepts, such as osmosis in biology and molecular structures in chemistry. Others disagree. Sadler and Tai (2007) performed a large-scale study of eight thousand college students and found that sequence did not predict grades in introductory science courses, but the number of years of high school mathematics did. While the best sequence for high school science education is debatable, both camps recognize the critical role that background knowledge plays in acquisition of new learning. Sophisticated schemata of physics and mathematics appear to be associated with higher levels of science learning (Martin et al. 2004; Sadler and Tai 2007). In other words, students' ability to connect background information, in this case mathematics with science, is important for their achievement. When they are missing information or have only bits and pieces of disconnected information, learning is interrupted.

The inability to apply background knowledge can interfere with the kind of deep analysis adolescent learners are required to perform. Wolfe and Goldman (2005) studied the relationship between background knowledge, reasoning, and explanation of forty-three sixth-grade students from five different classrooms who read two conflicting accounts about the fall of the Roman Empire. The researchers asked each participant to describe his or her background knowledge about the Roman Empire (the students had received six to eight weeks of instruction during the school year), then had each read the two documents and think aloud. The researchers noted the types of associations and reasoning the students used to understand the documents, including irrelevant associations, such as "My family visited Rome last year" (481). Interestingly, nearly 50 percent of the background knowledge associations drawn by these students did not contribute to text understanding. The authors stated that "although they may have provided the reader with a vague sense of topic familiarity, they did not further understanding of the historical event" (494). But more to our point, students who appropriately utilized their background knowledge scored higher on measures of reasoning for the task (Wolfe and Goldman 2005). In other words, despite having been taught about the Roman Empire by their social studies teachers and developing a general sense of this time in history, their ability to exhibit higher-order reasoning was not a given, and a significant percentage of the students did not effectively use their background knowledge to help them understand. And that's where teachers come in. We have to constantly guide students in developing and activating relevant background knowledge.

We witness this "right church, wrong pew" phenomenon in classrooms frequently. For example, groups of our ninth-grade students were analyzing fables to determine the moral of the story. One of the groups was assigned "The Tortoise and the Hare." In their discussion, Andrew shared his background knowledge about turtles. He said:

> I know a lot about turtles. They are cold-blooded and live on every continent, except Antarctica. Turtles have pretty good eyesight and a really good sense of smell. Their shell even contains nerve endings so that they can feel things on their shell. They are one of the oldest kinds of reptiles and have outlived other species that have gone extinct. Their breeding cycle is complicated but all turtles lay eggs on the land.

While correct and interesting, the background knowledge that Andrew activated wouldn't help him analyze the moral of the fable his group was assigned. In fact, his thinking about this information might even have interfered with his ability to analyze the text. He was thinking about the biological world while the assignment required that he think about the metaphorical world. Having said that, you can probably guess that Andrew understood that turtles are generally considered slow movers. And that tiny bit of background knowledge would have probably been of more help for this unit on fables than his considerable knowledge of the species.

■ Transferable

As previously stated, students must possess an organized schema of knowledge, and they must utilize it appropriately to understand new information. The third condition for learning, as described by the National Research Council, is the ability to transfer background knowledge to novel situations. Of course, transfer is dependent on good first teaching, without which transfer isn't possible. You might have been engaged in transfer while reading this chapter as you have applied the familiar metaphor of the teenager's backpack to help you reach a new understanding for this framework for learning.

Transfer, the *application* of new learning, is the ultimate goal of our teaching, yes? It's why we set our alarm clocks and get to school each morning, hoping that our students will take all the footballs of knowledge we toss their way and run with them into their lives. But let's be honest: it's one of the biggest challenges we face each day, too. We have found ourselves on more than one occasion bemoaning the fact that we modeled and demonstrated how to do something in our teacher education courses and gave our students lots of opportunities to replicate it in the university classroom. But when it came time for our students to use what they knew in a novel situation such as their own classrooms, they struggled. The research on establishing sub-goals has been very helpful to our own teaching practices for promoting transfer. Establishing subgoals involves chunking the steps necessary to complete a task (e.g., Catrambone 1995). Think of it as organizing minischemata. The evidence is that novices have difficulty transferring background knowledge to novel situations because they attempt to memorize a sequence rather than pay attention to the conceptual aspects of the task (Atkinson, Catrambone, and Merrill 2003). When the steps are grouped into conceptually similar chunks, transfer improves.

This was demonstrated in a study of 112 statistics students, who were taught about two types of statistical hypothesis tests (t-tests and ANOVA) using either a model that emphasized computational steps or one that emphasized conceptual ones. While both groups performed similarly when asked to solve equations that were closely matched to the ones done in class, those students taught under the conceptual condition were able to apply their skills at a higher level when faced with novel situations that did not closely replicate what they had done in the classroom (Atkinson, Catrambone, and Merrill 2003). There is research evidence that knowledge is transferred in pieces, not as a wholly formed abstract concept (diSessa 1993; Wagner 2003).

For example, in their tenth-grade science class, students learned a great deal about earth science and the difficulty of planetary investigations from Dr. Donna Ross, their teacher. They also studied robotics, mechanics, and data collection. Donna created a project that would challenge students to transfer their understanding. Their assignment was to build a planetary explorer that would gather the type of data they would need to describe this previously unknown place. Each team built a computer-controlled rover that would collect the information it wanted to analyze. Students maneuvered their rovers into one of several four-foot cubes covered with sheeting. Using optical cameras on the rover, the student teams could view the landscape inside the cube. They used robotically controlled arms to collect soil and rock samples. The planetary rovers also included measurement instruments for gauging temperature and humidity to determine whether water might be present. After guiding the rover out of the unknown planetary space, each team then had to assemble the data and analyze it to make predictions with supporting evidence about its composition and characteristics. By creating a project that emphasized conceptual knowledge rather than the completion of a defined set of steps, Dr. Ross gave her students an opportunity to transfer their background knowledge to a new situation. (See Figure 1.1.)

Figure 1.1 *Students working on robotics*

■ Three Reasons to Pay Attention to Background Knowledge

It is not enough to acknowledge the conditions necessary for background knowledge to be useful to support new learning. We want to be sure that we build your background knowledge about the importance of, well, background knowledge. Therefore, let's consider the impact of background knowledge on comprehension, vocabulary, and memory systems.

Background Knowledge Affects Comprehension

Let's shift gears by beginning with a scenario and then examining the research. Consider the way a lack of background knowledge affected one learner and how he helped himself.

Not too long ago, Doug wanted to learn more about the brain. Having just lived through the decade of the brain (so named because of vast research done throughout the 1990s) and not knowing much about this amazing organ, Doug decided to enroll in a neuroanatomy seminar. Proud of himself, Doug went to the bookstore to buy the required text for this graduate class. The first chapter, "Introduction," was incomprehensible to Doug. Despite his best efforts—including underlining, highlighting, and adding margin notes—he did not understand the text. He was about to give up on the class when a high school teacher reminded Doug that there was a very good explanation of basic neuroanatomy in the high school biology book. Doug checked a copy out from the school library and read up. Feeling more confident, Doug returned to his class the following week and tried again. The class lasted two hours and forty minutes, most of which was confusing for Doug. However, when the instructor discussed the four lobes of the brain, Doug was with her. He had the background knowledge necessary, because of his reading of the high school biology book, to engage in this part of the class.

Motivated by this momentary success, Doug stopped at the bookstore on the way home. Looking through the store for an accessible book, Doug stumbled on *The Complete Idiot's Guide to Understanding the Brain* (Bard and Bard 2002). This book provided the background knowledge Doug needed for several weeks. In addition to developing his background knowledge, he was learning labels (vocabulary) for the knowledge. Searching online for additional reading material, Doug found *Clinical Neuroanatomy Made Ridiculously Simple* (Goldberg 2007). This book provided the next level of information Doug needed to continue his studies.

Doug also accessed a number of nontraditional sources of information. For example, he watched more than one hundred YouTube videos on the human brain (search, for example, for "brain surgery" or "brain anatomy"), viewed the five-DVD series The Secret Life of the Brain, and tested himself using a number of Web-based quizzes (see www.vectors.cx/med/apps /cranial.cgi). By developing his background knowledge and vocabulary, Doug was able to pass this graduate class with the grade of A–. And if you're thinking that unlike many of our students, Doug was highly motivated, you're right. But that motivation, in and of itself, did not ensure that Doug learned. He still had to develop and activate relevant background knowledge to ensure that he passed the class.

Of course, there are students in middle and high school classrooms who don't have Doug's motivation. Motivation and attention are critical issues in learning (e.g., Guthrie and Wigfield 2000), and we recognize that there are specific things that teachers can do to influence motivation, but we have recently begun asking ourselves about the role of background knowledge and motivation. When students don't have background knowledge, new content seems overwhelming and learning tasks make them feel incompetent. Taken together, this has to dampen motivation. After all, how many of us are motivated to do things that are very hard for us and make us feel incompetent? Unfortunately, this becomes a vicious cycle in which motivation is further reduced as students have less background knowledge for the next task, and so on and so on.

The literature base confirms Doug's experience with background knowledge. As the National Reading Panel noted, readers "access their background knowledge to construct meaning from the text" (2000, 2-107). Like Doug, "children read and comprehend text by utilizing their linguistic and background knowledge combined with their word reading skill. When word reading skill is somewhat weaker, children can rely more heavily on their knowledge about the subject and memory for what they have read to still make sense of the text" (2-128).

The National Reading Panel report reminds us that we really need to consider the role of background knowledge in reading comprehension from two aspects. The first is the topical knowledge directly related to the text (Alexander, Kulikowich, and Schultze 1994). For example, given a reading about the impact of global warming on marine life, a student who knows a lot about penguins is at an advantage compared with a student who does not. The second is background knowledge of the way the text itself is structured. That same penguin-wise student loses some of her advantage if she doesn't have a strong footing in the differences between reading a narrative text and reading one that is informational (Goldman and Rakestraw 2000).

The RAND Reading Study Group (2002) describes reading comprehension as an interaction between the reader, the text, and the task. Background knowledge plays a role in each of these aspects. The most obvious is the reader, who brings "his or her cognitive abilities . . . motivation . . . interest in the content . . . knowledge . . . and experiences" to the act (xiii–xiv). Each of these is further affected by the text, which varies in difficulty according to the previously noted factors. Finally, the ability of a reader to comprehend is changed according to the task, which includes not only the demands but also the reader's knowledge of how to complete it (RAND Study Group 2002).

This is not to suggest that reading comprehension just happens; it is far from a passive act. Accomplished readers take an active stance, setting the purpose in their mind, comparing what they read with what they know, and noticing when their understanding breaks down (e.g., Paris, Wasik, and Turner 1991). They must also know how to use the background knowledge they possess when reading text (which is conditionalized), because this is not a given, either. Inferring is an aspect of reading comprehension that occurs as an interaction between the reader's background knowledge and the text. McKoon and Ratcliff demonstrated that most readers infer rather superficially (at the sentence and paragraph levels) and that "goal-directed, purposeful inferences" across larger pieces of text "do not occur unless the reader is well practiced" (1992, 463). The strongest readers are able to draw on both their topical knowledge and their understanding of text structures to infer in more sophisticated ways (Crain-Thoreson, Lippman, and McClendon-Magnuson 2004).

The need to attend to background knowledge is even more pronounced for English language learners. As García (1991) noted, English language learners typically have less background knowledge relevant to topics in English texts or tests. As would be expected of any learner asked to perform in a new language, English language learners have difficulty with questions that rely on background knowledge. It isn't that they lack the background knowledge, but rather that converting what they know to fit the academic language discourse of a discipline can present too large of a leap (Zwiers 2007).

Finally, online reading comprehension is emerging as a new arena for the study of the importance of background knowledge. Coiro and Dobler (2007) devised an ingenious study to examine this more closely. They identified the 11 strongest readers among a group of 150 sixth-grade students and analyzed the ways they used background knowledge, inferring, and monitoring to locate and understand online information. They discovered that the most skilled online readers not only utilized their topical and text structure background knowledge but also applied their understanding of how web pages and Internet search engines worked. In other words, print-based background knowledge was not enough; digital background knowledge was also essential.

To summarize, students need background knowledge of the topic, background knowledge of the format of the print-based or digital text, and a plan for how to utilize both if they are to understand at sufficiently high levels for learning complex content. But have you noticed how much of what you've just been reading about depends on your vocabulary knowledge? Although ubiquitous in the educational world, terms like *reading comprehension*, *inference*, and *cognitive ability* represent the type of academic language unique to our profession. In addition, the word *ubiquitous* in the previous sentence might have caused you to slow down just a bit as you calculated its meaning and remembered that it means something is every-where at once. In the same way, background knowledge and vocabulary are inexorably linked.

Background Knowledge Is Articulated Through Vocabulary

Consider the vocabulary of technology you have absorbed in the last decade. You've moved from owning a *cell phone* to a *PDA* (personal data assistant), you've gone from learning how to *email* to sending a *text message*, and it's likely that you have a passing understanding of what your computer's *hard drive* does and how to use a *search engine*. These terms are fairly ordinary at first glance, but each stands for a host of concepts. Take *cell phone*, for example. *Phone* is shorthand for *telephone*, a communication device that allows people to talk to one another by converting sounds into electrical impulses that are sent through electrical wires. A receiver in the handset of the telephone converts those signals back into sounds the human brain can recognize. The addition of the modifier *cell* represents an added layer of complexity. *Cell* can mean a living thing or a compartment. In this case, *cell* is a shorthand term for the longer word *cellular*. A cell phone is also a communication device, but it operates through a different technology than a *landline phone*. The cells are small geographical areas of about ten square miles that transmit the radio waves (not electrical impulses) from one handset to the next.

The purpose of this discussion is not to enlighten you on the nuances of cell phone technology, but rather to illustrate how vocabulary is a proxy for conceptual knowledge. Further, vocabulary knowledge is nested within larger concepts and links related concepts together. Depending on your knowledge of cell phones and computers, you might explain how *instant messages*, better known as *IM*, are similar to and different from *text messages*. Much like a tree that separates into limbs and branches, your schema of communication technologies is represented by vocabulary that serves as a placeholder for what you know.

Of course, most of us learned the technical words related to cell phones because they are rooted in our culture. We learn what is valued. One of the problems we face in school is that students often fail to see the social desti-nation, or even relevance, for their hard work in science, social studies, or mathematics.

As you might expect, vocabulary is closely correlated with background knowledge (e.g., Marzano 2004). Studies of language development with preschoolers show that the volume of word knowledge a child possesses upon entry to school is a strong predictor of achievement (Hart and Risley

1995). Similar results were obtained in a study of more than seven thousand sets of twins in the United Kingdom, where researchers found that environment made a greater contribution to language ability and reading ability than genetics (Harlaar et al. 2008). The snowball effect of negatively affected reading achievement is clear as students are expected to obtain more of their learning from text. Those who start behind have tremendous difficulty catching up with their peers. Lack of vocabulary knowledge also interferes with a student's ability to read fluently, resulting in slower and more labored experiences that ultimately influence volume (Samuels 2002).

The relationship between background knowledge and vocabulary doesn't stop there. Vocabulary knowledge correlates to academic achievement as measured by grades and standardized tests (Stahl and Fairbanks 1986). It can manifest itself in writing tests that measure academic discourse skills (Myhill 2005). And it should come as no surprise that it has a direct effect on world language learning (Hammadou 1991). A student's ability to explain, write about, and converse academically is expressed through her vocabulary knowledge because of its representative quality.

So reading comprehension and vocabulary are closely associated with background knowledge because they represent two sides of the same coin—receptive and expressive language abilities. A third factor now emerges. A learner must always be able to store and retrieve knowledge in a fluid and fluent fashion if it is to be useable; that is, he must have strong memory systems.

Background Knowledge Involves Memory Systems

The human brain is a complex and fascinating organ that is still not very well understood. Despite decades of research, the brain hasn't yet yielded its innermost secrets. What we do know about the brain, however, especially when combined with behavioral research, can help us improve teaching and learning.

For our purposes here, we'll focus on current thinking about memory, as memory is directly related to background knowledge. In essence, when we activate background knowledge, we're activating a range of memories. When we build background knowledge, we're essentially adding memories.

Not too long ago, researchers thought of memory as a structure or location and spent a great deal of time trying to find memory centers. Today we think of memory as process. Interestingly, there is evidence that memory storage is rather haphazard, meaning that people store different memories in different parts of their brains. While two people might have had the exact same experience, they probably stored that experience in different locations based on different pathways. This process, in turn, affects how easy it will be for those two individuals to retrieve the memory.

To understand the role of memory in background knowledge, we have to consider the fallible nature of memory and the brain's attempt to make meaning from fragments of sensory experience. Bartlett articulated this challenge back in 1932:

> Remembering is not the re-excitation of innumerable fixed, lifeless, and fragmented traces. It is an imaginative reconstruction, or construction, built out of the relation of our attitude towards a whole active mass of organized past reactions or experience, and to a little outstanding detail which commonly appears in image or in language form. It is thus hardly ever really exact, even in the most rudimentary cases of rote recapitulation, and it is not at all important that it should be so. (213)

Understanding that memory is a construction or reconstruction process, and one that is venerable to error, is important for teachers interested in background knowledge. It's just not that easy to tell students what they need to know. Building memories that students can use (retrieve) is the hallmark of quality education and is what this book is about. Throughout the chapters in this book, we provide examples of teachers who do exactly this; they develop students' habits of mind (Costa and Kallick 2009), extend their funds of knowledge (González, Moll, and Amanti 2005), and create a culture of thoughtfulness (Brown 1991).

Types of Memory

Memory researchers have worked to classify the various types of memory (e.g., LeDoux 2002). There is general agreement about two major divisions, or chunks, of memory: declarative and nondeclarative. Declarative memories are those that can be easily expressed in a sentence that makes a statement. For example, "Ocean water tastes salty" or "Water consists of hydrogen and oxygen." Also known as explicit memory, declarative memory can be subdivided into two categories: episodic and semantic. The ocean water example is episodic because it relates to experiences and events, whereas the hydrogen and oxygen example is semantic as it relates to facts. Both kinds of declarative memory are processed by the hippocampus, a structure deep within the brain. It seems that the hippocampus is critical in the formation of declarative memory and, if damaged, results in an inability to form or retain new memories. Parenthetically, the hippocampus is one of the first areas damaged in Alzheimer's disease.

Nondeclarative memory, also known as implicit or procedural memory, is associated less with the hippocampus and more with the sections of the brain that house specific sensory inputs. For example, how to swing a bat is associated with the motor cortex, whereas recognizing a melody is associated with the temporal lobe. Nondeclarative memories involve routines, skills, and behaviors that cannot be expressed in a declarative way. Nondeclarative memories do not require conscious attention or recall. For example, walking is a nondeclarative skill that most of us don't have to think about.

Memory
Formation
To help you organize the information we have already presented and the information that follows, Figure 1.2 provides a graphic representation of memory ability. As you can see, the types of memory are in the center of

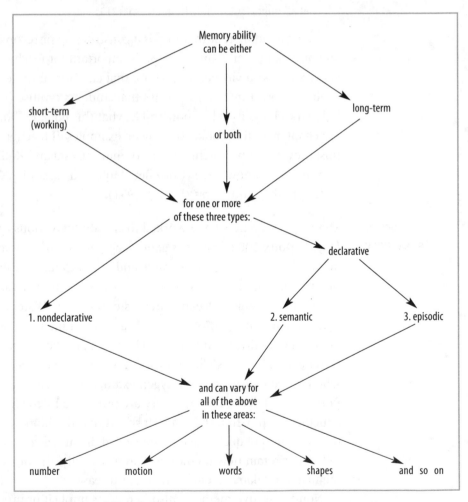

Figure 1.2 *Memory ability*

the illustration. The bottom of the figure indicates the various ways that memory can be expressed. The top of the graph indicates that memories begin as either short-term (working) memory or long-term memory.

Howard explains memory formation with an analogy to photography:

> Forming a chunk of memory is like making a photograph. Regard photography as a three-stage process: (1) capturing the image on light-sensitive film, (2) developing the film with chemicals, (3) fixing the image permanently with chemicals. A similar process happens in memory-chunk formation: capturing the chunk (immediate memory), developing it (short-term memory), and fixing it (long-term memory). (2006, 535)

Immediate memory, also known as sensory memory, is extremely short-term and subject to significant filtering. Consider all of the sensory information bombarding your brain as you read this paragraph. Your body is sensing the texture of the clothes you wear, how hard the chair is that you're sitting in, the sounds around you, the smell of dinner cooking, some hunger pains, and thousands of other bits of information. Most of this will be discarded, but some of it will enter the immediate memory system for action or further storage.

Short-term memory, often now called working memory, allows us to temporarily store and manipulate information. Again, much of the information that enters short-term memory is filtered or forgotten. If you've heard that humans can process about seven bits of information at a time, you're thinking of the work done with working memory. Miller (1956) demonstrated that people learn most efficiently when information is chunked into groups of seven (plus or minus two, depending on the person). More recently, Cowan (1998) suggested that Miller's "magic number" be revised from seven to four, based on the fact that some types of information are much harder to process than others. Cowan suggested that four was a more reasonable target for memory tasks and one that educators might consider when planning instruction.

Both immediate and short-term memory are fairly easy to grasp. Both involve the collection and rapid analysis of sensory information. Long-term memory is where things get a bit more confusing. It seems that long-term memory is stored all over the cerebral cortex. Somehow the hippocampus communicates with the cerebral cortex and memories are stored. But this takes time, attention, and often repetition. As Medina notes in his book *Brain Rules*, "the way to make long-term memory more reliable is to incorporate new information gradually and repeat it in timed intervals"

(2008, 147). This has clear implications for building and activating background knowledge. We have to be much more purposeful about memory formation and ensure that students have opportunities to cycle through information several times, in different ways, if they are to learn. Dina Burow, a colleague who teaches advanced math in high school, has taken on this challenge and invites her students to revisit the same information several times over the course of a class meeting. She develops and activates students' background knowledge as they create graphs with their bodies, play with adding fractions before factoring polynomials, and debate the best way to solve problems.

But here's an interesting finding from memory research: Learning a new motor skill requires between five and six hours, as the brain has to transfer from temporary storage to long-term storage (Shadmehr and Holcomb 1997). This involves all kinds of chemical reactions and changes in blood flow, but if this process is interrupted by an attempt to learn a different motor skill, problems result and permanent learning does not occur. While this research is focused on motor skills and we don't know if it applies to nonmotor learning, there are interesting implications. Specifically, Shadmehr and Holcomb recommend that new learning be followed by practice with familiar routines so that the brain has time to consolidate information.

Remembering   While the previous sections have focused on building background knowledge, remembering is the key to activating background knowledge. There are essentially three ways to aid memory: intend, file, and rehearse (Minninger 1984). But these ideas aren't new. As Yates (1966) noted, Erasmus named the same three keys in 1512 when he wrote, "Though I do not deny that memory can be helped by places and images, yet the best memory is based on three important things: namely study [rehearse], order [file], and care [intend]" (127). Yes, in fact, the world has known for almost five hundred years that there are specific ways to remember things.

But why is it that we sometimes don't activate the memories that we have? Or why do our students have difficulty activating their memories—memories that we have worked so hard to facilitate? Schacter (1999) identified seven basic areas of concern (which he called sins): transience, absentmindedness, blocking, misattribution, suggestibility, bias, and persistence. "The first 3 sins involve different types of forgetting, the next 3 refer to different types of distortions, and the final sin concerns intrusive recollections that are difficult to forget" (182). A description of each of these seven can be found in Figure 1.3.

1. *Transience*: Specific memories of facts and events become less accessible over time. This is known as long-term forgetting, as memories that were once stored are lost. One way to prevent transience is to regularly retrieve and rehearse experiences or memories.

2. *Absentmindedness*: Some forgetting occurs because we did not pay significant attention to the information in the first place. Unlike with transience, with absentmindedness, information is not coded because we simply didn't attended to it. This is common when we complete routine tasks automatically as our attention is focused elsewhere.

3. *Blocking*: Sometimes memories are simply unavailable, but the individual knows that the information is there. Often expressed as tip-of-the-tongue experiences, blocks can occur in both episodic and semantic memory. Blocking is often resolved with time and may be helped when attention shifts to a different topic, giving the brain time to find the memory.

4. *Misattribution*: As Schacter noted, the first three are omission errors. Misattribution is a source error in which people name the wrong source for the idea or memory. While common, this memory error is especially problematic in eye-witness accounts, as individuals are convinced their memories are accurate.

5. *Suggestibility*: Like misattribution, suggestibility is an error of commission. The difference in suggestibility is that the error occurs because of misleading information provided during a recall attempt. For example, a leading question might allow someone to incorporate information provided by others into a memory.

6. *Bias*: Memory, both in terms of storage and retrieval, is significantly influenced by preexisting knowledge, values, and beliefs. Accordingly, memories can be altered by an individual's current beliefs. In essence, a memory is changed to fit with current knowledge.

7. *Persistence*: The final sin of memory, as Schacter calls them, involves remembering something that you wanted to forget. This often occurs during stressful times. In fact, there is evidence that failing to forget can be more traumatic than forgetting.

Figure 1.3 *Sins of memory*

The key to remembering is repetition and use. In 1949, Donald Hebb suggested that neurons that fire together simultaneously are more likely to fire together in the future. According to Hebb's theory, these networks are created and established through experiences and subsequent use. Siegel rephrased Hebb's theory and simply stated, "Neurons that fire together, survive together and wire together" (Siegel 2000, cited in Wolfe 2001, 76). And that's what we're hoping for as teachers: neurons that wire together to create memories for students that they can activate throughout their lives.

■ Conclusion

Just think about the experiences of students in a typical classroom and the range of background knowledge they each have. Some students have been to the beach and others have not. Some have read *Harry Potter* while others have not. Children who live in poverty may have never been on vacation to the Grand Canyon. Children who live in the city might have never walked through the woods and built their knowledge of nature. And some children have never visited a museum or had parents read books to them at night. While it is true that their lived experiences are likely different, there are things teachers can do to activate and build background knowledge.

Yet background knowledge is too often neglected in our push to raise test scores despite the fact that we know background knowledge is a critical component of comprehension. It's related to vocabulary and word knowledge, which every teacher knows is important. And further, background knowledge affects every child as it involves working and long-term memory. Background knowledge simply has to become an instructional focus if we want to help students make sense of school. We will lose a generation of learners if we don't act now.

Placing Background Knowledge in Daily Teaching

WHEN WE GIVE WORKSHOPS AND MAKE THE CASE for ramping up students' background knowledge, we often hear teachers in the audience literally sighing. They ask: "How can you possibly jam this stuff into an already overpacked curriculum? I went into teaching because I love social studies; how can I be expected to do all this front-loading? Why should I take on this burden because students' previous teachers didn't get them up to speed?" The answer to these questions has less to do with adding to your teaching than it does with becoming more strategic about how you teach. We have each been teaching for more than twenty years, but it's only in the last few that we've realized just how critical it is to teach with the learning cycle in mind—that is, to teach with an instructional framework that supports how humans learn. Too often in middle school and high school, teachers default to quite a lot of lecture and students' learning shuts down. Instead, we need to

- *assess* what students already know;

- *plan lessons and activities* that build students' background knowledge; and

- *design ways to activate* students' knowledge by having them *interact* with content.

We need to go far beyond reading textbooks in a same-old, same-old manner to have students manipulate and apply information, wrestling with it enough that they come to own it, so that it becomes permanent understanding. Along the way, we hope that students engage in critical and creative thinking and gain new types of literacy skills, including those of the twenty-first century. We have this image of throwing open the windows and doors of a beach cottage that has been locked up all winter—it's time to let fresh breezes blow into our teaching, time to whip things up so they don't remain stale. As cliché as it sounds, the Internet has changed everything; we have to think globally. We now use a structured approach to teaching that has redefined our practice.

■ A Structured Approach to Teaching

Even when students possess a rich trove of background knowledge, it lies fallow in school unless we provide opportunities for students to bring it forth. Our structured approach to teaching is based on the gradual release of responsibility model of comprehension instruction (Pearson and Gallagher 1983), with an emphasis on group work that stems from collaboration between students (see Figure 2.1).

We draw on the work of Vygotsky (1978) and others in our emphasis on a recursive cycle of modeling, scaffolding, small-group coaching, and individual coaching—all with an eye to helping each student toward independent learning. The elements of structured teaching include the focus lesson, guided instruction, collaborative learning, and independent learning (Fisher and Frey 2008). Each phase of instruction includes opportunities to activate, build, and apply background knowledge. We'd even go so far as to say that effective teaching *is* building background knowledge—you can't have one without the other.

Background Knowledge Within an Instructional Framework

- *Focus Lesson*: The teacher establishes a purpose and models the actions and processes used to complete a task. This is done by thinking aloud so that learners can witness how the teacher accesses her background knowledge to

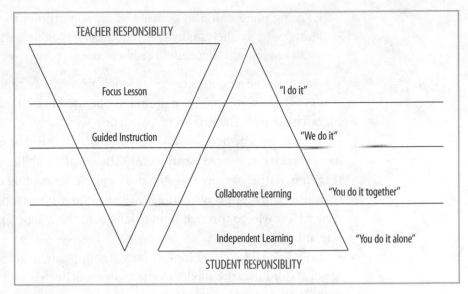

Figure 2.1 *A structured model for teaching*

solve some challenge, whether it's puzzling a way through complex text or solving a math equation. In hearing an expert's moment-by-moment cognitive decisions, students in a sense share the teacher's consciousness.

- *Guided Instruction*: Students assume some of the cognitive load to apply their background knowledge and new learning to a task that is novel, but closely parallel, to the one modeled by the teacher. While the learner takes the lead, the teacher is close by to scaffold the student's understanding by helping with the tricky parts. This may include assisting the learner in accessing the relevant background knowledge needed. Guided instruction can be done individually, in small groups, or with the whole class. The key lies in the strategic use of cues, prompts, and questions that allow students to do more of the work.

- *Collaborative Learning*: This phase of learning is a linchpin because it gives the students opportunity to coach one another as they clarify their understanding of a targeted process or action. Students work in small groups to complete a task designed to consolidate background knowledge with new learning. The key is that the group work should be productive and build for transfer, and it should feature both individual and group accountability measures.

- *Independent Learning*: Learners utilize all their resources to complete a task designed to reinforce an action or process. This reinforcement is intended to develop fluency and automaticity so that what was initially new learning now becomes part of the student's background knowledge. The independent learning phase can also be used as an opportunity to build background knowledge, as when students engage in wide reading activities like sustained silent reading or independent reading.

Notice we've described the phases of instruction as a recursive cycle; we want to underscore that they should not be used in a strictly sequential or hierarchical way. The phases of instruction will likely occur in an order other than the one described here. Our experience is that applying the model in lockstep unnecessarily limits the teacher's ability to build understanding. Rather, we use this model as a guide for making decisions in our own teaching about how learners will encounter opportunities to build conceptual knowledge through interactions with the teacher, the materials, and one another.

Now let's take a closer look at how eighth-grade social studies teacher Mimi Oxford uses the model as she assesses, activates, and builds her students' background knowledge.

■ Activating and Building Background Knowledge in One Classroom

Mimi Oxford's eighth-grade course focuses on U.S. history and geography from the Revolutionary War until World War I. The overarching themes of the state history content standards for this grade level are *growth* and *conflict*, and the teacher knows that these represent core knowledge for the year. As such, she designed her curriculum to continually return to these two themes. Over the course of the year, she wanted her learners to understand that this period of U.S. history was marked with the successes and failures brought about by the decisions of leaders and citizens. During the first week of school, she introduced these two terms to her students, and they constructed visual maps to reflect their understanding of these terms. These remained on display for the entire year, and the teacher added new terminology to build their schema for this vital vocabulary.

The unit of instruction she taught for the next few weeks focused on the time period from 1763 to 1791, when the colonists were increasingly feeling the effects of an inequitable economic and political distribution of power between themselves and the British government. She wanted her students to understand that the actions taken by individuals and groups to change this ran the gamut from statesman-like to revolutionary, and that the precedence for protest and freedom of expression in our country could be traced to these early historical roots.

Name: _____ Period: _____ Date: _____

Directions: Think about your own reactions to these statements and place a check mark in the column that best matches your opinion. There are no right or wrong answers.

What's Your Opinion?

SA = Strongly Agree   A = Agree   D = Disagree   SD = Strongly Disagree

Statement	SA	A	D	SD
A patriot is heroic.				
Sometimes the only thing left to do is fight for what you believe in.				
The American Revolutionary War could have been avoided if both sides had compromised on taxation.				
All the colonists were in support of the war.				

Figure 2.2 *Social studies opinionnaire*

Mimi knew that her students were all over the map in terms of their level of background knowledge. A few had already startled her with their command of history, and a few had startled her with how little they knew about this country's origins. She wanted to get a general read on the entire class—find out about their impressions of this time period in general—so she administered a short opinionnaire (see Figure 2.2) that contained four statements. She assured them that there were no right answers. She also wanted to learn about their content knowledge and selected a pivotal paragraph from their textbook (Appleby et al. 2003) to use as a cloze assessment. She chose this passage because it contained previously learned information that they would need to leverage as background knowledge, as well as new content (see Figure 2.3).

Based on the results of her assessments, Mimi knew that the majority of her students saw conflict as necessary to produce change, and that most of them also thought that fear of physical retribution motivated many Loyalists. She knew this because nearly 80 percent of her students wrote *lives* or *heads* for number 9 in the sentence "Some remained loyal to __7__ king because they were __8__ who would lose their __9__ as a result of __10__ Revolution." She

Choosing Sides

As American colonists heard about these battles in Lexington, Concord, and Bunker Hill, they faced a major decision. Should they join the __1__ or remain loyal to __2__? Those who chose to __3__ with Britain, the Loyalists, __4__ not consider unfair taxes __5__ regulations good reason for __6__. Some remained loyal to __7__ king because they were __8__ who would lose their __9__ as a result of __10__ Revolution. Others were people __11__ had no been part __12__ the wave of discontent __13__ turned so many Americans __14__ Britain. The Patriots, on the other hand, were determined to fight the British to the end—until American independence was won.

1. rebels	10. the
2. Britain	11. who
3. stay	12. of
4. did	13. that
5. and	14. against
6. rebellion	15. Britain
7. the	16. and
8. officeholders	17. with
9. positions	

Figure 2.3 *Cloze assessment from textbook passage*

knew that she would need to build on these concepts in order to connect them to the themes of growth and conflict.

So as a next step, Mimi planned a lesson wherein she placed students in groups of five and assigned them the role of either Loyalist or Patriot. Since she knew that the students did not possess much specific background knowledge about these groups, she gave them a list of reasons why the Loyalists and Patriots aligned themselves to their positions. She had students read and discuss the position statements, then create a broadside on poster paper to hang up in the "town square"—the school hallway. Students discussed why Loyalists and Patriots might see war with Britain as a good or bad idea and then listed these reasons for others to see. For example, one Loyalist group's broadside said, "We are the business owners of the town. If we can't trade with Britain and other countries, we won't have anything to sell you." A group of Patriots prepared a broadside that read, "When we were a poor colony, Britain left us alone. They just ignored us. Now that we are getting more rich, Britain is interested all of a sudden. They just want to put their hands in our pockets." The broadsides were posted in the hallway, and all the groups read each one.

Mimi then asked her students to return to the classroom with their broadsides to continue their work. "You've had a chance to read about the ideas of others who support your cause and the arguments of those who are opposed. What will you add to your broadside to make it more persuasive?" she asked. The Loyalist group added this statement, gleaned from another broadside: "If we stay loyal, the king will reward us with more business. We will get richer by not fighting." The Patriot group added this information: "You can't trust the king because he makes promises he doesn't keep. Remember the Intolerable Acts?"

The following day, Mimi began class with a think-aloud reading of *Give Me Liberty! The Story of the Declaration of Independence* (Freedman 2000). It's a dynamic text that would further her students' understanding quickly, and she modeled for students the way she used her own background knowledge to solve for comprehension and vocabulary. She projected the book on the document camera and opened to the first page. "Follow along with your eyes and your mind while I read. I'll stop from time to time to tell you what I'm thinking about," she explained. She read to them from the first chapter, "The Night the Revolution Began," and looked at the picture on the left page.

"I read the title, and my eyes immediately popped over to this painting," she explained. "The caption says that it's about the destruction of tea at Boston Harbor, and I can't help but notice that there are a lot of cheering people on the dock. The people on board the ship look like Native Americans, but I know they're not. I am using my background knowledge to remind myself that they were really Patriots disguised as Mohawk Indians."

A few minutes later, she arrived at a passage about the reasons for the Boston Tea Party. She read, "The colonists objected to paying King George's taxes without having a voice in Parliament. They called it taxation without representation. And while the tax on tea was a small one, just three cents a pound, it was regarded as a symbol of British tyranny" (2).

"I've heard about Parliament before. That's the name of the group of representatives in Britain that made laws. I learned about Parliament when I read about England taking over the colonies from the Dutch one hundred years earlier. I recall now that Parliament also came up with the plan to ship prisoners from English jails to the colonies. Hmmm . . . it seems like Parliament didn't always have the colonies' best interests in mind when they made decisions."

On the next page, she read a paragraph about the conduct of the protestors on the night of the Tea Party. "Several thousand people had gathered to watch in silent approval from the wharf. Aboard the ships, great care was taken that the protest be carried out with discipline. Nothing but tea was disturbed, and 'not the least insult was offered to any person,' John Andrews reported" (3).

"This was something I wasn't aware of until I read it here," she said. "To look at the picture and think about the word *party*, you'd think that it would have been pretty rowdy. But in truth they carried out the protest very respectfully. Maybe they are using *party* to mean celebration and not a big, loud event."

Later in the same lesson, Mimi assigned some students to independent reading while she met with others for guided instruction. The readings she selected for this unit were meant to build background knowledge among students who had gaps in their understanding and to reinforce what they had been learning during this unit. She chose short readings using the MAS Ultra—School Edition database because it was designed for school libraries and offers Lexile levels for many of the readings. A list of the readings Mimi selected can be found in Figure 2.4. In addition to print readings, she also

Reading Selection	Length	Ease of Reading	Lexile
Fleming, T. 2006. "The Not-So-Hidden History." *Boys Life* 96 (9): 44–47.	4 pgs.	Easy	800
Fleming, T. 2006. "The Treaty That Rescued a Revolution." *Boys Life* 96 (8): 40–45.	6 pgs.	Easy	840
Pitt, W. 1767/1997. "Speech on the Stamp Act." British House of Commons, www.history.org/almanack/life/politics/pitt.cfm	3 pgs.	Easy	900
Calkins, V. 1993. "Radical Revolutionary Samuel Adams." *Cobblestone* 14 (9): 20–22.	3 pgs.	Average	1030
Rosenfeld, R., and N. M. Mattila. 2007. "Learning the Soldier's Life." *Cobblestone* 28 (8): 7–10.	4 pgs.	Average	1070
Ferling, J. (2007). "100 Days That Shook the World." *Smithsonian* 38 (4): 44–54.	9 pgs.	Difficult	1190
Schwarz, F. D. (1999). "1774." *American Heritage* 50 (3): 110-1–11.	2 pgs.	Difficult	1190
Kaye, H. J. (2005). "Founding Father Thomas Paine." *American Heritage* 56 (5): 66–68.	3 pgs.	Difficult	1390

Figure 2.4 *Independent reading selections*

found a WebQuest for students to use ("Acts of Parliament, in Defense of the British," at http://smith.quicktel.com/quests/british_laws.htm), which she bookmarked on the classroom computers because she wanted to reinforce the yearlong themes of growth and conflict. "I can't have them only knowing one side of the story," she explained to us. "Every argument has two sides, and the British had their own motives for ruling as they did. That's where conflict springs from—strongly held beliefs of both sides."

While other students read these selected readings, she met with small groups of students to read and discuss a passage from the textbook on the Intolerable Acts. From past experience, she knew that students often struggled with the terminology, so she developed a graphic organizer for them to use (see Figure 2.5). As the students read and discussed the passage, she

Name of Act	What Was It?	Why Did It Make Colonists Angry?	Results
Boston Port Act	Closed port of Boston after Tea Party.	It punished everyone instead of just the ones who did it.	Colonists from far away sent supplies, and this helped them learn to work together.
Massachusetts Government Act	Britain took over Massachusetts government.	Now they couldn't rule themselves.	Town meetings couldn't be held without permission.
Administration of Justice Act	British could have trials in England.	It cost too much for people to go to the trials.	Made it easier for Britain to win trials.
Quartering Act	British soldiers could stay in empty buildings.	They didn't like having soldiers hanging around.	This would be a part of the U.S. Constitution.
Quebec Act	Gave land to France west of Appalachian Mountains.	Pennsylvania and New York thought this was their land.	Made lots of Canadians friends with the colonists.

This is intolerable!

Figure 2.5 *Graphic organizer for Intolerable Acts*

reminded them to use the graphic organizer to not only name the acts but also consider why the colonists would be so angry about each new law. When Ari struggled to name the effects of the Boston Port Act, Mimi prompted him, "Reread these sentences here," pointing to the text. "Use what you know about how this text is organized to see if you can locate the effects." Ari began to reread, but Mimi sensed he was still unsure what he was looking for. "Look for a signal word that tells you about a result," she told him. He reread the section on the act and put his finger on the sentence "Parliament planned to isolate Boston with these acts. Instead the other colonies sent food and clothing to demonstrate their support for Boston" (Appleby et al. 2003, 139).

"Oh, yeah, I remember this now," Ari said, smiling. "The colonies didn't really help each other before. But now they were all ganging up on the bully," he remarked.

Remember our opening analogy of the teen with his backpack in Chapter 1? Think about how Mimi took the time to compel Ari to do some work on locating the information in the text. She could have just told him the effects of the Boston Port Act and moved on to another student, but she knew she needed to work with Ari in his zone of proximal development—nudging him one step closer to owning vital reading strategies.

Mimi continued to teach this unit about the time of conflict leading up to the Second Continental Congress' passage of the Declaration of Independence, so that by the time the students were learning about this foundational document, they understood that it represented the final break from Great Britain following a year of war that began at Lexington and Concord. Her students had learned about the personal sacrifices of citizens and politicians and held a deeper appreciation for the personal risk that the signers assumed. What had once been new knowledge for them was now becoming background knowledge, as she modeled how she interpreted political cartoons from this time period from America and Britain. The last one she showed them was a contemporary one, drawn by political cartoonist Steve Breen for the *San Diego Union-Tribune* (see Figure 2.6). Using the iconic painting by John Trumbull portraying the moment when the document was signed, Breen had imposed a speech bubble that read, "If they're so patriotic, where are their flag pins?" Judging by the laughter, Mimi knew the students were drawing on their background knowledge of the event. She asked for someone to explain why it was amusing.

"Well, it's funny because those guys were the original patriots—the OPs," Kurt explained while the class giggled. "Those guys went through a lot just

Figure 2.6 *Political cartoon*

to get there. You weren't a patriot because you wore some pin. You were a patriot because you stood up for what you thought was right." Mimi knew that it was time to add this idea to their chart on growth, because they were moving beyond surface-level facts to understand the significance of this event in the life of a young country.

■ Conclusion

This extended portrait of one teacher's classroom represents a snapshot of the type of teaching and learning that occurs in classrooms across the country every day. Students arrive with varying levels of background knowledge, and effective teachers find creative ways to assess what they know and do not know so that they can teach for deep understanding, not just superficial facts. Like Mimi Oxford, they assess their own curriculum to determine what are the core understandings for the unit and what is the incidental knowledge that students will need to learn. They organize their curriculum to return to these core understandings, as with Mimi's themes of conflict and growth. Effective teachers understand that activating background knowledge is more than just starting a lesson with a warm-up to provoke interest, and they instead choose instructional routines that activate the right background knowledge learners will need for the task. As with Mimi, they build background knowledge systematically, using approaches like wide reading, think-alouds, and experiential learning. In addition, they utilize methods for organizing their schemata so that resultant learning doesn't look like a messy closet of jumbled details that can never quite be located. In other words, effective teachers have ways to ensure that our metaphorical teenager has his backpack when he needs it. And finally, effective teachers pay attention to the skills learners in the twenty-first century will need as they navigate information sources that come at them as rapidly as the changes of a complex world.

No one said that it was simple, but it is possible. In the next chapter, we describe methods for assessing both the curriculum demands and our students' background knowledge to determine how the two might best interface. In Chapters 4 and 5, we share ideas for activating and building background knowledge so that students can acquire new knowledge. And in Chapters 6 and 7, we move beyond conventional thinking about background knowledge to include current conversations about critical literacy and new literacies. When background knowledge becomes a lens through which we plan and deliver instruction, students learn and remember in amazing ways.

Teacher as Archaeologist

Assessing Background Knowledge

NOT LONG AGO, WE MET WITH A NINTH GRADER about an essay he'd turned in. We were concerned that he might have plagiarized it. "Tell us about your writing process," we began. "How do you give credit to the ideas of others? When do you know when a sentence or set of ideas is your own, and when might it be plagiarized?" The student quite sincerely explained his process and that he hadn't plagiarized, because he'd selected synonyms using the right-click feature on his computer. He even demonstrated it for us: he copied a passage from an Internet source and pasted it into a document, then changed most of the adjectives, adverbs, and verbs. He went on to explain that his previous teachers had taught him to paraphrase by "using [his] own words" and that's exactly what he was doing. We knew right away he was telling the truth.

We share this story with you because we could have made a critical error at that moment. If we had failed to take the time to assess this student's prior understanding of plagiarism, we could have rushed to judgment, giving him a zero for the assignment, making a call home to his parents, or taking some sort of disciplinary action. However, the conversation revealed what he knew and did not know about writing, and the result was a teaching opportunity. We're happy to report that he left with a more nuanced understanding of how to use information in essays correctly.

This story also helps us make the point that to assess your students' background knowledge, in a way you have to wear the hat of an archaeologist. You'll need to ask yourself three questions:

1. What do students need to know?

2. What do they currently know?

3. How does this inform my instruction?

Peeling back the layers of understanding necessitates a careful and deliberate approach that can reveal the bones of students' content knowledge. The process also allows the teacher to determine where the young learner's understandings might be weak or incomplete and what needs to be done to strengthen them. To borrow the language of the field of archeology, it requires survey (knowing where to look), excavation (bringing it to the surface), and analysis (examining it closely).

The National Research Council's Center for Education explains the same principles:

> Every assessment, regardless of its purpose, rests on three pillars: a model of how students represent knowledge and develop competence in the subject domain, tasks or situations that allow one to observe students' performance, and an interpretation method for drawing inferences from the performance evidence thus obtained. (2001, 2)

Assessment of background knowledge in principle does not differ from the more familiar formative measurement events common in classrooms. We like to think of background knowledge assessment as the most formative of all assessments because when it is done correctly or in earnest, it truly guides and informs instruction *starting at the planning stage* and carrying through lesson delivery and student feedback.

■ Surveying Background Knowledge: Knowing Where to Look

The starting point for assessing background knowledge begins with the teacher's ability to identify the foundational understandings needed to comprehend new information. As noted in Chapter 1, new learning is best constructed on a bedrock of existing knowledge. Therefore, it is essential for teachers to name for themselves the information a learner must call upon. Quite simply: *What are the nonnegotiable, core concepts my kids need to have from the get-go in order to proceed with my unit?* This can be challenging, because sometimes we presume they know things they don't. This is what we mean by peeling back the layers. For example, let's take a fairly current situation: If some of your high school students don't know about the stock market crash of 1929 and the Great Depression, their understanding of early 2009's newspaper headlines comparing the two periods of financial crisis is going to be much thinner than yours or ours. To have a meaningful discussion of the pros and cons of President Obama's plans for rebuilding the nation's infrastructure, you'll probably need to build background knowledge about FDR's Works Progress Administration efforts first.

Remember the old Gap ads? "For every generation there's a Gap." As we assess our students, our mantra might be "For every generation there's a knowledge gap." Think of it! Students in middle and high school have no recollection of a world without wireless communication, gene therapy, mainstream media's embracing of cultural and ethnic diversity, the war on terrorism, or reality television. The 1960s civil rights movement, antiwar protests, cultural upheaval, the women's movement—none of these is part of their psyches and knowledge banks. Sure, maybe it was their parents' history, but the operative word is *history*. Consider, then, how this might affect students' understanding of the following events:

- Ernest Shackleton's ill-fated *Endurance* expedition in the Antarctic in 1914
- Crick and Watson's 1953 discovery of the double-helix shape of DNA
- the Cold War and twentieth-century conventional warfare
- Frank Stockton's 1884 short story "The Lady or the Tiger"
- Hilary Rodham Clinton's bid for the presidency in 2008
- Barack Obama's ascension to the presidency of the United States in 2009

Here's the real challenge, though: deciding what is the superficial background knowledge that you can easily explain and don't need to teach more fully and what "enduring understandings" (Wiggins and McTighe 2005, 17) you want students to accrue. You know your content pretty well, so our experience is that once you start thinking along these lines, you'll be able to zoom in on the hot spots of the content pretty quickly. No archaeologist begins digging in a random spot. Instead, she possesses a rationale for the selection of the location based on what she is looking for, and researches it thoroughly before ever beginning to dig. In the same way, a teacher must examine the critical features of the content to be taught and then extract the most useful background knowledge possible. The method we use to determine what is core knowledge and what is incidental knowledge is based on four criteria:

1. *Representation*: Is it essential?

2. *Transmission*: Can it be easily explained, or must it be taught?

3. *Transferability*: Will it be used for future understanding?

4. *Endurance*: What will be remembered after the details are forgotten?

For the last criterion, we thank Grant Wiggins and Jay McTighe for their work on enduring understandings. A chart of this decision-making model can be found in Figure 3.1.

Core Knowledge		Incidental Knowledge
The information is foundational to understanding the main concepts.	*Representation*	The information may be interesting, but it's peripheral to the main concepts.
Requires multiple exposures and experiences.	*Transmission*	Can be explained or defined easily (using a label, fact, or name).
Will be needed again to understand future concepts	*Transferability*	Specific to this concept; unlikely to be used in the future.
Will be remembered after details are forgotten.	*Enduring*	Details and specifics are not likely to be recalled later.

Figure 3.1 *Decision-making model for identifying core and incidental knowledge*

Surveying a Text in Ninth-Grade English

English teacher Cora Roberts wanted to use the Edgar Allan Poe short story "The Cask of the Amontillado" with her ninth-grade students but was discouraged from doing so by her colleagues who told her that "the kids really don't seem to like it much." Cora learned that the unit they designed began with building background knowledge on Carnival celebrations and its costumed participants. Cora decided that she needed to identify the types of background knowledge her students would need to understand this nineteenth-century story in a more systemic way. She brainstormed a list of elements and then divided them into two categories: core background knowledge and incidental background knowledge. As she reread the story, she realized that the Carnival celebration could be explained in a straightforward way, as could the traditions of wearing a costume, so she placed this in the incidental category, along with several other facts. She examined the items listed under "Core Knowledge" and recognized that a pattern was emerging—the importance of pride, revenge, and family honor (see Figure 3.2).

She understood that the enduring themes of revenge and murder would resonate with her students but also knew that their understanding would hinge on a critical piece of information: the symbolism of the coat of arms described in the story. She began by displaying drawings of such heraldry, including the use of a motto. "Many families used symbols to describe the strength of their people in times of war," she began. "Look at this eagle. It symbolizes a swift and sudden death, like when an eagle attacks its prey."

Incidental Knowledge	Core Knowledge
Carnival celebrations	Knowledge of the era regarding maintaining pride and reputation
Amontillado is a kind of wine.	The importance of revenge to resolve grievances
Wine cellars and catacombs are underground.	Family reputation through the generations
Freemasons is a secret society.	Symbolism of the Montresor coat of arms
	The unreliable narrator
	Impunity: getting away with something with no punishment

Figure 3.2 *Cora Robert's list of background knowledge for "The Cask of the Amontillado"*

She showed several others, including a lion, a cross, and an axe, and then distributed a drawing of the coat of arms in the story. This one featured a snake being crushed by a human foot as the snake strikes. "Take a look a this coat of arms. Talk at your table about what you think this symbolizes." Most agreed that the snake is a traditional symbol of evil of the most deadly sort and that the bite might be a poisonous one. They concurred that this would be the coat of arms of a family that stamped out injustice in the world.

Cora wasn't finished. "Now tell me what it means when you add the motto 'Nobody provokes me with impunity.' The word *impunity* means that you get away with something without being punished. Is it the snake or the human who represents this family?"

This question prompted quite a discussion in class. Raymond made a connection to the Harry Potter books he'd read in middle school. "Maybe this family is like Slytherin," he offered. "You know, the evil ones."

However, Sarah disagreed. "I think the foot is what's most important," she stated. "That's the real action in this coat of arms. This family sees its duty as crushing the wrongdoer. They have no mercy."

All agreed, however, that the ambiguous use of the pronoun *me* was intriguing. "I guess it could go either way," Raymond conceded. Although they were not yet using the word *impunity* in their academic language, Cora noted that they were already beginning to consider punishment as a point of honor. She explained that the coat of arms belonged to the family of the narrator of the story and told them that this would be key to understanding him and his actions. By building this core background knowledge, the teacher readied her students for the first paragraph:

> The thousand injuries of Fortunato I had borne as I best could, but when he ventured upon insult I vowed revenge. You, who so well know the nature of my soul, will not suppose, however, that gave utterance to a threat. At length I would be avenged; this was a point definitely, settled—but the very definitiveness with which it was resolved precluded the idea of risk. I must not only punish, but punish with impunity. A wrong is unredressed when retribution overtakes its redresser. It is equally unredressed when the avenger fails to make himself felt as such to him who has done the wrong. (Poe 1846/2002, 231)

"Whoa! I can already see that dude's face!" exclaimed Raymond. "This Fortunato guy is gonna get whacked!"

Cora knew that she was not finished building background knowledge with her students. As her lessons progressed, she would discuss the emphasis on maintaining family honor in the early nineteenth century, and they would also learn about the literary device Poe pioneered—the unreliable narrator. But this first foray into the dark wine cellar with the menacing narrator had already been a success, because she had focused her students' attention on revenge and honor as a core understanding of the piece.

As teachers, we often find ourselves at a crossroads; we can cave to the temptation to water down our teaching because we think kids won't understand a story and therefore avoid challenging texts, or we can recognize the disservice we are doing to them by failing to analyze, develop, and activate their background knowledge such that they engage with interesting texts that will help them understand themselves and the world around them.

Surveying Geometric Concepts in Middle School Mathematics

Of course, conceptual knowledge is not always text based; take mathematical principles, for example. Many of us will recall we learned somewhere along the way that the sum of the interior angles of a triangle is 180 degrees. Chances are that you memorized this fact through repeated exposure. But do you know *why* this is true? And furthermore, would understanding why it is so quicken the pace for learning?

Antonio Ventura, a sixth-grade mathematics teacher, planned a unit on the properties of two-dimensional figures. In particular, his students needed to be able to solve for complementary and supplementary angles of triangles. Antonio also knew that students who rely on memorizing concepts without understanding them more deeply quickly become confused when confronted with plane geometry.

Antonio decided that he must first establish a rationale for why the interior angles of a triangle always add up to 180 degrees. He knew that budding mathematicians who understand core concepts are able to apply this knowledge correctly in novel situations. He gave each student a sheet of scrap paper from the copy room and a pair of scissors. After introducing the concept, he told them that they would be able to prove whether he was correct or not using the materials on their desks. "I can't wait to find out what you discover," he told them. He instructed them to cut out a triangle (right, equilateral, or isosceles) and then to snip the three angles off. "Now line those three clipped angles up so that they form a straight line," he said. The gasps began almost immediately.

"How can that be, Mr. V?" asked Gregory. "Does it always work?"

"Try it again for yourself," the teacher encouraged. "Use a different triangle this time. And don't bother to cut it," he said. "Just tear off the corners." (See Figure 3.3).

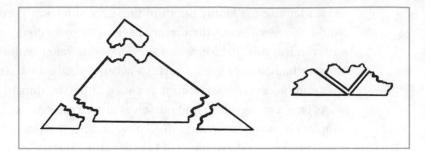

Figure 3.3 *Antonio Ventura's angle activity*

Again and again, the students tried variations, only to discover that the angles, no matter how irregularly separated from the triangle, could always be reassembled as a straight line. "Now let's talk about the properties of a straight line, which you've already learned. How many degrees in a straight line?" asked Mr. Ventura.

"One hundred eighty degrees!" the class replied.

"Right! Now use your mathematical logic here. The three angles of the triangle always seem to make a straight line. So how many degrees are the sum of the three angles?" He cupped his ear for effect.

"One hundred eighty degrees!" they chimed in with even more enthusiasm.

"There you go! Now choose three angles from the same triangle and write 'fifty degrees' on one and 'sixty degrees' on another. Add that up to figure out what the third one equals."

The students quickly got to work solving this problem. As the first of them arrived at an answer, he directed them to talk to a partner about the solution. Within two minutes, everyone in the class arrived at the correct answer of seventy degrees.

Antonio's next lessons would continue to build on this major concept as his students mastered solving for complementary and supplementary angles. And he couldn't wait to show them in a few weeks that the same principle applies to polygons (which are really composed of two triangles) and that a polygon's angles always total 360 degrees.

■ Excavating Background Knowledge: Bringing It to the Surface

Once you've discovered and brought your enduring understandings to the surface, it's time to set them next to what your students currently know and don't know. Teaching is about sleuthing out the most meaningful ways to get from students' current knowledge to enduring understandings. We recently read an article in the *New York Times* that reminded us of our teacher-as-archeologist analogy (Haederle 2009). It featured archeologist Patricia Crown, who solved the mystery of the Pueblo jars. She and others had studied these decorated clay vessels excavated from the mesas of New Mexico for years and years and hypothesized their use as drums or sacred objects. Using her background knowledge about pottery and the trade routes of the Mayans, and collaborating with both an expert on Ecuadorian and Columbian history and a biochemist from the Hershey Company, who detected theobromine, a cacao marker, in the clay, she was able to prove the jars were actually used for ritualized chocolate drinking practices during special feasts! We love this story because it shows how background knowledge in real life gets put to use and how even experts can get sidetracked by details that lead them to stick to wrong hunches. We share the story at this juncture because it underscores the responsiveness of this archeologist—to arrive at the truth, the enduring understanding of those clay jars, she had to negotiate what she knew with others' current understandings (or lack thereof) and probably do plenty of backtracking and regrouping along the way, much as a responsive teacher does as she builds students' knowledge.

Responsive teaching—and responsive sleuthing of what students know—is closely linked, of course, to surveying the content for enduring understandings. Both require recognition on the teacher's part of what must be understood by the learner. Two of the most effective means for assessing what students know and don't know are anticipation guides that feature misconceptions and opinionnaires that elicit opinions through value statements.

Unearthing Misconceptions

Cognitive scientists have long been fascinated with understanding the role of misconception in learning. This interest consists of two subsets: identifying misconceptions associated with disciplines and determining how misconceptions can be corrected so that new learning can occur.

Misconceptions should not be confused with factual errors. A simple factual error, for instance, a belief that the Great Wall of China can be seen from space, can usually be cleared up with direct explanation (check out Wikipedia if you hold this factual error). Misconceptions, on the other hand, represent a fundamental flaw in knowledge and reasoning that then spills over into other facets of learning. Examples of misconceptions in various content areas can be found in Figure 3.4. Students use these misconceptions to explain other phenomena, leading to a cascade effect. New learning

Content	Misconception
Life Science	• The water in the water cycle today is the same water from millions of years ago. • Organisms higher on the food chain are predators of all organisms below it. • Muscle cells push and pull.
Physical Science	• Faster-moving objects have a larger force acting upon them. • Two objects traveling at the same velocity will also have the same acceleration.
History	• World War II in Europe was waged against Germany (omitting Italy and Russia). • The American Civil War was fought to free enslaved people. • Failure to understand the progression of time in multiple locations simultaneously (the snapshot effect).
Mathematics	• The absolute value of a number is a positive number (rather than the distance from zero). • Variables stand for specific objects (e.g., $3d + 2c$ means three dollars and two cents). • Identification of a shape is based on appearance rather than properties.
English	• A sentence must never begin with *And* or *But*. • A sentence should never end with a preposition. • Formal academic writing should never include the word *I*.

Figure 3.4 *Commonly held misconceptions in secondary subjects*

predicated on a shaky foundation will topple, as evidenced in the well-known documentary *A Private Universe*. In this film, Harvard faculty members and newly minted graduates provided elaborate (and incorrect) explanations for why there are seasons or why there are phases of the moon (hint: it's not because Earth casts a shadow). Despite their command of academic vocabulary and excellent educational experiences, twenty-one of the twenty-three people who appear on the film had failed to master a fundamental understanding of Earth's movement in relation to the Sun. (To view this documentary, go to www.learner.org/resources/series28.html.)

The first step in uncovering student misconceptions is to possess a working knowledge of the common misconceptions associated with your discipline. For example, many physics teachers know that students come to them possessing all kinds of misconceptions that end up affecting learning. One of the most common is the belief that the faster an object moves, the

Biology	Weber University departments.weber.edu/sciencecenter/biology%20misconceptions.htm
Physics	University of Montana Student Difficulties in Physics Information Center www.physics.montana.edu/physed/misconceptions/index.html
Algebra	University of California–Irvine https://eee.uci.edu/wiki/index.php/*Algebra_and_Functions
Earth Science	U.S. Geological Survey www.usgs.gov

Figure 3.5 *Teacher resources on misconceptions*

larger the force is that acts upon it. Tom Brown and Jeff Crowder, authors of the website for the Physics Misconception Center at the University of Montana, note that "some students believe in their heart of hearts that force is proportional to velocity" and that this is a particularly difficulty notion to dislodge. Their website contains multiple-choice questions and explanations on physics topics and is useful for teachers who are creating questions meant to surface these misconceptions. Similar websites for other discipline areas can be found in Figure 3.5.

An anticipation guide is an effective way to determine the misconceptions held by students (Tierney, Readance, and Dishner 1995). Usually, you administer one near the beginning of a lesson or unit of instruction. It gives you formative assessment data to plan your instruction, and it draws the learner's attention to assumptions he holds. To create one, devise five to ten statements constructed for true-or-false responses. You can either deliver the questions verbally or present them as a written handout. Don't grade them; just use them as a barometer of class understandings and as prompts for an initial discussion on the topic at hand. Often, it's useful to pose the statements again near the end of the lesson or unit, when students can provide justification for true statements and a reasoning for why false statements are incorrect. This provides you with excellent pre- and postlearning quantitative data, as well as qualitative information about the extent to which the learner understands key concepts.

Anticipation Guides in Earth Science

Ellen Wexford's sixth-grade earth science class was about to begin a unit on earthquakes and she knew from experience that despite being residents of an earthquake-prone region, her students held many misconceptions about tectonic activity. For instance, many of them believed that a megaquake on the San Andreas Fault could cause California to break off from the continent. Ellen recognized that even though to some degree her students knew it was an urban legend, it nonetheless signaled that their understanding of earthquakes was, well, a bit shaky. So she constructed an anticipation guide (see Figure 3.6) that would be useful to her and her students. She had made guides in the past that she realized were flawed because they focused on isolated facts (incidental knowledge) rather than core knowledge. "When I first started using these a few years ago, I would include items about the names of faults, or knowing how many earthquakes occur each year worldwide. Those are important and they'll be taught in the unit. They don't necessarily let me know anything about misconceptions that will interfere with new learning," she told us. The one she now uses was developed through a survey of the textbook materials and outside sources, especially the U.S. Geological Survey's Earthquakes Hazard Program (earthquake.usgs.gov /learning/faq.php).

We asked her what she intended to discover about her students' background knowledge. "I chose each item because it correlates to the core knowledge they will need for this unit," she explained. She went on to describe that core knowledge:

1. Rocks possess a degree of elasticity that results in elastic strain energy. When the elastic strain is too much, an earthquake will occur.

2. Earthquake damage continues after the event is over, especially in populated areas where man-made structures are lost.

3. Magnitude measuring systems work on an amplitude scale, not on an intensity scale.

4. Earthquakes originate in Earth's crust, usually less than one hundred miles deep.

5. The physics of seismic waves results in transmission through the mantle and core to the other side of Earth. Sensitive machines are capable of measuring these waves, even though they cannot be felt by humans.

6. The San Andreas Fault in California is a slip-strike fault between the North American and Pacific plates. Movement between the plates is roughly northwest, not apart (as in California breaking off).

"I give the guide to them on the first day of the unit, after we've watched some video footage of earthquakes and their aftermath. This activates their prior knowledge and experiences and gives us a good foundation for

Name: _____ Period: _____

Directions: Read each statement and answer true or false.

Before	Statement	After
	1. Rocks stretch and flex during an earthquake.	
	2. Damage continues to occur after the earthquake ends because of landslides, fires, and tsunamis.	
	3. An earthquake of magnitude 6.0 is twice as strong as one that is magnitude 5.0.	
	4. Earthquakes begin deep in Earth's core.	
	5. Seismic waves from an earthquake can be measured on the other side of Earth.	
	6. California might break off from the continent because of a large earthquake.	

After: Explain why each statement is true or false.

1. _____

_____

2. _____

_____

3. _____

_____

4. _____

_____

5. _____

_____

6. _____

_____

Figure 3.6a *Anticipation guide for earth science*

Name: _____ Period: _____

Directions: Read each statement and answer true or false.

Before	Statement	After
	1.	
	2.	
	3.	
	4.	
	5.	
	6.	

After: Explain why each statement is true or false.

1. _____

   _____

2. _____

   _____

3. _____

   _____

4. _____

   _____

5. _____

   _____

6. _____

   _____

Figure 3.6b *Blank anticipation guide*

discussion," Ellen continued. "I collect them and analyze them by student so I get a good sense of who knows what. I am often surprised to find out who the experts are! It also allows me to create new learning experiences for those who have already mastered this core knowledge." She went on to describe the experiences she would create for students during the unit, including labs on elasticity and seismic wave measurement. "When I'm nearing the end of this unit, I give them their own anticipation guides back again, so that they can answer the items again and notice how their knowledge has grown. I also require them to explain why they know what they know."

She explained that she doesn't ask them for their reasoning when she first hands out the anticipation guide, based on prior experience. "I found that most of them don't know why they know something initially. My students seemed to struggle with this, and I'd mostly get replies like 'Because it is.' That's not very helpful. By the end, though, I want them to be able to support their position with evidence. I suppose that's me using my own background knowledge!" she concluded with a grin.

Ellen's use of an anticipation guide works well in content areas like science, history, and mathematics, but this tool is a bit more difficult to use in English and the humanities. That's because misconceptions, per se, are less clear in these disciplines. Rather, students are drawing on their personal experiences to formulate opinions. These are often informed by belief systems, cultural traditions, and values. For that reason, labeling such beliefs as misconceptions would be inaccurate. However, it is helpful to learn about the opinions of students in order to craft new learning. An opinionnaire, an instrument used widely in social sciences research, is useful for locating the perspectives of students on topics that don't have a right answer (Smagorinsky, McCann, and Kern 1987). Like anticipation guides, they consist of five to ten statements. In contrast, they feature a Likert-type scale ranging from strongly agree to strongly disagree. We do not include a neutral response since this is not consistent with the intent of this assessment (Fisher et al. 2007).

Opinionnaires in World History

Ron Sato was looking forward to welcoming his new tenth-grade world history students and carefully planned his early assessments for the first week of September. Although his content draws on an enormous foundation of factual knowledge, he recognizes that the discipline also involves interpretation and analysis. "I teach students who come from all over the world," he explained. "The background knowledge they use to understand history is shaded by their own experiences and cultures. I need to know some things

Name: _____ Period: _____ Date: _____

Directions: Think about your own reactions to these statements and place a check mark in the column that best matches your opinion. There are no right or wrong answers.

What's Your Opinion?

SA = Strongly Agree   A = Agree   D = Disagree   SD = Strongly Disagree

Statement	SA	A	D	SD
History is the winner's story.				
A representative democracy is the best form of government.				
Revolution is necessary for political change to occur.				
Exploration and industrialization have done more harm than good in Africa and Asia.				
The human cost of war is too great to justify military conflict.				
The world became a safer place after World War II.				
Nation building is the obligation of the victor.				

Figure 3.7a *Opinionnaire in world history*

about their views of the world." Ron developed an opinionnaire to learn about their perspectives so he could integrate these into his instruction (see Figure 3.7). "I've chosen these statements because they align with major units I'll be teaching this year," he said. "I'll also use a version of each of these as a central issue for the units. I want them to wrestle with these complex issues."

He went on to describe how he planned on using each during the school year:

 *Unit 1:* Is history only the winner's story?

 *Unit 2:* Winston Churchill said that democracy is the worst form of government, until you consider the others. Was he right?

Name: _____ Period: _____ Date: _____

Directions: Think about your own reactions to these statements and place a check mark in the column that best matches your opinion. There are no right or wrong answers.

What's Your Opinion?

SA = Strongly Agree   A = Agree   D = Disagree   SD = Strongly Disagree

Statement	SA	A	D	SD

Figure 3.7B *Blank opinionnaire*

- *Unit 3:* You say you want a revolution—but at what cost?

- *Unit 4:* Did the Industrial Revolution make life better or worse?

- *Unit 5:* War: What is it good for?

- *Unit 6:* Was World War II worth it?

- *Unit 7:* Can you build a nation when it's not yours?

"None of these are answered simply," Ron explained, "and I want them to appreciate the complexities of these questions. For example, kids at this age are ready to protest nearly anything, but they don't necessarily think through the costs of their actions. I want them to more fully understand why some revolutionaries have used violence to overthrow governments, while others have staged bloodless coupes. And what about civil disobedience? Under what circumstances has it been used to great effect?"

The teacher went on to describe how he would use the results of the opinionnaire. "First of all, it's a good temperature check for me. Each period is a bit different, and this is one of the ways I can see that. I even share the class averages for each statement with them so that they can begin to see the ways their opinions are different and the same as their peers. I also gain some insight into the individual belief systems of students. A student who is a recent refugee from a war-torn area of the globe is going to see the world differently from the kid who's rarely been outside of his own neighborhood. I survey them again at the end of the year, and they're always amazed at the ways their opinions have shifted or not shifted at all. Regardless, they all have a lot more knowledge to use to support their opinions. And isn't that a major goal in world history?" Of course, we know that effective teachers informally assess the accrual of background knowledge daily, via discussion, writing-to-learn prompts, and projects. Not a day should go by when the teacher is fuzzy on how the day's teaching was understood by students.

■ Examining Background Knowledge: Tools for Analysis

As we have noted, assessing background knowledge involves closely examining what students know *to inform instruction*. While anticipation guides and opinionnaires are useful for the broad strokes of assessment, finer tools are needed for systematic analysis of individual students' background knowledge. Many school districts require that certain assessments be administered at the beginning of the school year in order to obtain information about the skills each student possesses. For instance, many primary teachers collect reading assessment data using tools such as the Benchmark Assessment System (Fountas and Pinnell 2007), which is individually administered. The student reads a book while the teacher records errors on a scoring sheet. After the reading, the teacher and child discuss the content of the story. The teacher analyzes the resulting data using the guidelines included with the instrument to gain a sense of how the student uses graphophonic, semantic, and syntactic cueing systems to read and understand text. Teachers of older students may rely on informal reading inventories such as the Qualitative Reading Inventory—4 (Leslie and Caldwell 2005). These normed narrative and expository grade-level passages provide teachers with processes for assessing both silent and oral reading, as well as comprehension. Like the Benchmark Assessment System, these are individually administered.

However, these are much less common at the secondary level because of the class size of most classrooms. It is not possible for teachers to administer so many individual assessments that are this time-consuming; for the most part, they are reserved as diagnostic tools for students who are working well below grade level. Fortunately, there are instruments and techniques that can provide secondary teachers with a level of analysis for assessing what students know.

Meta-comprehension Analysis in English

Shaqura Williams, a middle school English teacher, understands that her classroom is a place for students to learn about themselves as readers. She structures her course around literature circles (Daniels 2002) in order to differentiate texts to better meet the range of abilities in her class. Of course literature circles or book clubs can be used across content areas. Our colleague Maria Grant has groups of her chemistry students read in clubs like this to deepen their understanding of scientific discovery.

But back to Shaqura. She typically begins each class with a shared reading and think-aloud so that she can model her expert use of comprehension strategies, show how she comprehends new vocabulary, and demonstrate how she uses text structures and text features to aid in her understanding of the text (Fisher, Frey, and Lapp 2008). Her students then move to their literature circle groups, where they read and discuss a thematically related text using some of the same techniques modeled by their teacher. Given that the range of possible strategies is so large, Shaqura needed a way to analyze what her students did and did not need to have modeled. In addition, she wanted to determine their level of awareness, or metacognition, in order to better understand what they knew about themselves as readers.

Metacognition is a learner's ability to describe his thinking and to monitor it (National Research Council 2000; Schmitt and Hopkins 1993). It is also a marker of what divides the novice from the expert (Ericsson and Charness 1994). While a middle school reader might not be described as an expert, there is evidence that there is a strong link between metacognitive awareness and reading ability (Cross and Paris 1988). Shaqura decided to use a tool called the Metacomprehension Strategies Index (Schmitt 1990) to analyze the ability of her students to notice their own reading processes (see Figure 3.8). The MSI is a twenty-five-item assessment that can be administered in one session. Students respond to questions about their reading, choosing the best answer from a set of four.

After collecting the results of the assessment, Shaqura analyzed it using the interpretation guidelines suggested by the author. She created a spreadsheet that gave her results by period and by individual student, and then she used this information to plan her modeling. She also used the results to confer with individual students who were having difficulty calling upon comprehension strategies to read challenging text, allowing her to further differentiate her instruction during literature circles. Thus background knowledge, in this case about strategic reading, significantly influenced the content of what was taught to which students.

Cloze Assessment in Civics

The MSI is useful in an English class because it is reflective of the content taught. That being said, there isn't a similar instrument for every discipline. This doesn't mean that content knowledge can't be assessed in other ways. One of the most useful and easily analyzed assessments for determining background knowledge is the cloze procedure. Originally developed as a measure of determining readability of text (Taylor 1953), the procedure was soon being used to determine levels of comprehension (e.g., Shanahan, Kamil, and Tobin 1982).

A cloze procedure, so named because of the closure effect prompted by the task, consists of a teacher-selected passage of 250 words. Every fifth word is deleted, and the first and last sentences are preserved in their entirety so that the reader can draw on context. This means that a variety of words end up being deleted—articles like *a* and *the* as well as content vocabulary. Students read the passage and fill in the missing words. Scoring is straightforward as well, with most sources recommending that a word be marked as correct only if it is an exact match. This may seem counterintuitive, but it

Name:_____ Date: _____

Metacomprehension Strategy Index

Directions: Think about what kinds of things you can do to help you understand a story better before, during, and after you read it. Read each of the lists of four statements and decide which one of them would help you the most. Circle the letter of the statement you choose.

I. **In each set of four, choose the one statement that tells a good thing to do to help you understand a story better** *before* **you read it.**

1. Before I begin reading, it's a good idea to:
   A. See how many pages are in the story.
   B. Look up all of the big words in the dictionary.
   C. Make some guesses about what I think will happen in the story.
   D. Think about what has happened so far in the story.

2. Before I begin reading, it's a good idea to:
   A. Look at the pictures to see what the story is about.
   B. Decide how long it will take me to read the story.
   C. Sound out the words I don't know.
   D. Check to see if the story is making sense.

3. Before I begin reading, it's a good idea to:
   A. Ask someone to read the story to me.
   B. Read the title to see what the story is about.
   C. Check to see if most of the words have long or short vowels in them.
   D. Check to see if the pictures are in order and make sense.

4. Before I begin reading, it's a good idea to:
   A. Check to see that no pages are missing.
   B. Make a list of words I'm not sure about.
   C. Use the title and pictures to help me make guesses about what will happen in the story.
   D. Read the last sentence so I will know how the story ends.

5. Before I begin reading, it's a good idea to:
   A. Decide on why I am going to read the story.
   B. Use the difficult words to help me make guesses about what will happen in the story.
   C. Reread some parts to see if I can figure out what is happening if things aren't making sense.
   D. Ask for help with the difficult words.

6. Before I begin reading, it's a good idea to:
   A. Retell all of the main points that have happened so far.
   B. Ask myself questions that I would like to have answered in the story.
   C. Think about the meaning of the words that have more than one meaning.
   D. Look through the story to find all of the words with three or more syllables.

7. Before I begin reading, it's a good idea to:
   A. Check to see if I have read this story before.
   B. Use my questions and guesses as a reason for reading the story.
   C. Make sure I can pronounce all of the words before I start.
   D. Think of a better title for the story.

8. Before I begin reading, it's a good idea to:
   A. Think of what I already know about the things I see in the pictures.
   B. See how many pages are in the story.
   C. Choose the best part of the story to read again.
   D. Read the story aloud to someone.

Figure 3.8 *Metacognition Strategy Index (Schmitt 1990)*

9. Before I begin reading, it's a good idea to:
   A. Practice reading the story out loud.
   B. Retell all of the main points to make sure I can remember the story.
   C. Think of what the people in the story might be like.
   D. Decide if I have enough time to read the story.

10. Before I begin reading, it's a good idea to:
    A. Check to see if I am understanding the story so far.
    B. Check to see if the words have more than one meaning.
    C. Think about where the story might be taking place.
    D. List all of the important details.

II. **In each set of four, choose the one statement that tells a good thing to do to help you understand a story better *while* you are reading it.**

11. While I am reading, it's a good idea to:
    A. Read the story very slowly so that I will not miss any important parts.
    B. Read the title to see what the story is about.
    C. Check to see if the pictures have anything missing.
    D. Check to see if the story is making sense by seeing if I can tell what's happened so far.

12. While I am reading, it's a good idea to:
    A. Stop to retell the main points to see if I am understanding what has happened so far.
    B. Read the story quickly so that I can find out what happened.
    C. Read only the beginning and the end of the story to find out what it is about.
    D. Skip the parts that are too difficult for me.

13. While I am reading, it's a good idea to:
    A. Look all of the big words up in the dictionary.
    B. Put the book away and find another one if things aren't making sense.
    C. Keep thinking about the title and the pictures to help me decide what is going to happen next.
    D. Keep track of how many pages I have left to read.

14. While I am reading, it's a good idea to:
    A. Keep track of how long it is taking me to read the story.
    B. Check to see if I can answer any of the questions I asked before I started reading.
    C. Read the title to see what the story is going to be about.
    D. Add the missing details to the pictures.

15. While I am reading, it's a good idea to:
    A. Have someone read the story aloud to me.
    B. Keep track of how many pages I have read.
    C. List the story's main character.
    D. Check to see if my guesses are right or wrong.

16. While I am reading, it's a good idea to:
    A. Check to see that the characters are real.
    B. Make a lot of guesses about what is going to happen next.
    C. Not look at the pictures because they might confuse me.
    D. Read the story aloud to someone.

17. While I am reading, it's a good idea to:
    A. Try to answer the questions I asked myself.
    B. Try not to confuse what I already know with what I am reading about.
    C. Read the story silently.
    D. Check to see if I am saying the new vocabulary words correctly.

Figure 3.8 *Metacognition Strategy Index (continued)*

18. While I am reading, it is a good idea to:
    A. Try to see if my guesses are going to be right or wrong.
    B. Reread to be sure I haven't missed any of the words.
    C. Decide on why I am reading the story.
    D. List what happened first, second, third, and so on.

19. While I am reading, it is a good idea to:
    A. See if I can recognize the new vocabulary words.
    B. Be careful not to skip any parts of the story.
    C. Check to see how many of the words I already know.
    D. Keep thinking of what I already know about the things and ideas in the story to help me decide what is going to happen.

20. While I am reading, it's a good idea to:
    A. Reread some parts or read ahead to see if I can figure out what is happening if things aren't making sense.
    B. Take my time reading so that I can be sure I understand what is happening.
    C. Change the ending so that it makes sense.
    D. Check to see if there are enough pictures to help make the story ideas clear.

III. **In each set of four, choose the one statement that tells a good thing to do to help you understand a story better *after* you have read it.**

21. After I've read a story, it's a good idea to:
    A. Count how many pages I read with no mistakes.
    B. Check to see if there were enough pictures to go with the story to make it interesting.
    C. Check to see if I met my purpose for reading the story.
    D. Underline the causes and effects.

22. After I've read a story, it's a good idea to:
    A. Underline the main idea.
    B. Retell the main points of the whole story so that I can check to see if I understood it.
    C. Read the story again to be sure I said all of the words right.
    D. Practice reading the story aloud.

23. After I've read a story, it's a good idea to:
    A. Read the title and look over the story to see what it is about.
    B. Check to see if I skipped any of the vocabulary words.
    C. Think about what made me make good or bad predictions.
    D. Make a guess about what will happen next in the story.

24. After I've read a story, it's a good idea to:
    A. Look up all of the big words in the dictionary.
    B. Read the best parts aloud.
    C. Have someone read the story aloud to me.
    D. Think about how the story was like things I already knew about before I started reading.

25. After I've read a story, it's a good idea to:
    A. Think about how I would have acted if I were the main character in the story.
    B. Practice reading the story silently for practice of good reading.
    C. Look over the story title and pictures to see what will happen.
    D. Make a list of the things I understood the most.

Figure 3.8 *Metacognition Strategy Index (continued)*

Interpreting the Results of the Metacomprehension Strategies Index

The MSI is a measure of a student's use of strategies with narrative text. It may be read to the student or administered silently. The wording of the items can be substituted to reflect expository text. For example, you can replace the wording of item 2 to read:

Before I begin reading, it's a good idea to:
A. Look at the illustrations to see what the chapter will be about.
B. Decide how long it will take for me to read the chapter.
C. Sound out the words I don't know.
D. Check to see if the information is making sense.

Answer Key: These answers represent the best answers; items may include strategies that are somewhat useful but not as efficient for the situation described.

1. C	6. B	11. D	16. B	21. C
2. A	7. B	12. A	17. A	22. B
3. B	8. A	13. C	18. A	23. C
4. C	9. C	14. B	19. D	24. D
5. A	10. C	15. D	20. A	25. A

Figure 3.8 *Metacognition Strategy Index (continued)*

really does make scoring easier and consistent across students. The scale reflects the variation in word selection that will occur:

- *Independent Level*: 60 percent correct or above

- *Instructional Level*: 40 to 59 percent correct

- *Frustration Level*: 39 percent correct or below

Because a cloze procedure is easy to develop and score, it is ideally suited to content area classrooms. We recommend that cloze assessments be administered before instruction begins to ascertain background knowledge of students. If the text is drawn directly from reading materials the students will use, it can serve the dual purpose of measuring text readability as well as content knowledge. This is especially valuable when there is a wide range of reading ability in your classroom.

Aaron Grayson used a cloze assessment before each unit of instruction in his civics course. He selected a passage from the textbook, looking for a

Interpreting: The following item analysis is organized to more fully describe the types of meta-comprehension strategies tested.

Strategies	Items
Predicting and Verifying Predicting and verifying the content of a story promotes active comprehension by giving readers a purpose to read (i.e., to verify predictions). Evaluating predictions and generating new ones as necessary enhance the constructive nature of the reading process.	1, 4, 13, 15, 16, 18, 23
Previewing Previewing the text facilitates comprehension by activating background knowledge and providing information for making predictions.	2, 3
Purpose Setting Reading with purpose promotes active, strategic reading.	5, 7, 21
Self-Questioning Generating questions to be answered promotes active comprehension by giving readers a purpose for reading (i.e., to answer questions).	6, 14, 17
Drawing from Background Knowledge Activating and incorporating information from background knowledge contributes to comprehension by helping readers make inferences and generate predictions.	8, 9, 10, 19, 24, 25
Summarizing and Applying Fix-Up Strategies Summarizing the content at various points in the story serves as a form of comprehension monitoring. Rereading or suspending judgment and reading on when comprehension breaks down represent strategic reading.	11, 12, 20, 22

Figure 3.8 *Metacognition Strategy Index (continued)*

section that contained both new content and previously taught concepts. After preparing the passage, he distributed it to his students (see Figure 3.9 for an example from Remy et al. [2003]). "You're pros at this by now," he said to one class, "but I still want to remind you of some good strategies to use. Remember to read the passage all the way through before answering. That gives you some contextual clues. And remember that you can skip one and go back to answer it later," he continued. "Finally, remember that this isn't a test; this is part of your participation in the class. I use the results to get a good idea of what you know and don't know. Go ahead and begin."

Market Economies

Not all economic systems are alike. Some, like the one _1_ the United States, are _2_ on markets. Others, like _3_ , include far greater government _4_ . These different economies deal _5_ scarcity in different ways. _6_ societies face the basic _7_ of what to produce, _8_ to produce it, and _9_ whom to produce it. _10_ way these questions are _11_ determines a society's economic _12_ . In a pure market _13_ , these decisions are made _14_ free markets based on _15_ interaction of supply and _16_ . Capitalism is another name _17_ this system.

One of _18_ chief characteristics of a _19_ economy is that private _20_ —not the government—own _21_ factors of production. As _22_ recall, these factors include _23_ resources, capital, labor, and _24_ .

Because the factors of _25_ are in private hands, _26_ market economy offers a _27_ degree of individual freedom. _28_ make their own decisions _29_ what to produce, how _30_ produce it, and for _31_ to produce it. Driving _32_ decisions is the business _33_ desire to earn a _34_ . At the same time, _35_ make their own decisions _36_ what to buy.

In _37_ market economy, these decisions _38_ place in the market. _39_ and demand interact to set _40_ , and producers and consumers _41_ their decisions on prices.

_42_ market economy is decentralized. _43_ is, decisions are made _44_ all the people in _45_ economy and not by _46_ a few. The economy _47_ to run by itself _48_ no one coordinates these _49_ .

There are no pure _50_ economies in the world. In the United States, for example, government provides public goods such as defense and a system of justice.

1. in	18. the	35. consumers
2. based	19. market	36. about
3. China's	20. citizens	37. a
4. control	21. the	38. take
5. with	22. you	39. Supply
6. All	23. natural	40. prices
7. questions	24. entrepreneurship	41. base
8. how	25. production	42. A
9. for	26. a	43. That
10. The	27. high	44. by
11. answered	28. Businesses	45. the
12. system	29. regarding	46. just
13. economy	30. to	47. seems
14. in	31. whom	48. because
15. the	32. those	49. decisions
16. demand	33. owner's	50. market
17. for	34. profit	

Figure 3.9 *Cloze assessment in civics*

Students began reading the passage silently, and within a few minutes they were writing terms on notebook paper. Aaron chose this passage because it required them to use their background knowledge about factors of production, which they had covered in a previous unit. It also contained new information about market economies, which he had alluded to but not yet taught. In addition, he planned on analyzing the results of Antonio's work more closely than the rest. Because Antonio was new to the class, Aaron did not yet have a good sense of his reading ability or knowledge of civics, and this would be an ideal opportunity to find out about both. He was pleased with the content vocabulary that they would need to successfully complete it, with words like *entrepreneurship*, *supply*, *consumers*, and *production* missing from the passage. When he first began using the cloze procedure, he thought that it would be better if he chose the deleted words. However, he quickly discovered that the results from deleting every fifth word worked just fine. He made a mental note to include this passage again on the unit test, since that would give him some valuable postinstruction information to compare.

Of course, cloze procedures, like the other assessment tools we've discussed in this chapter, are not limited to use in the social studies classroom. Our colleagues in chemistry, Spanish, and art history have all used cloze to assess their students' background knowledge.

Interest Surveys in Biology

Interest surveys have been used in marketing research since the early twentieth century as a means for determining product design and advertising. They are widely used in assisting people with career choices, and corporations use them frequently with their employees to determine need and improve the workplace to increase retention. Yet outside of reading selections, interest surveys are rarely used in secondary education. Perhaps we are intimidated by what we may discover—what if they're not interested in our class? As well, we may feel as though we have little influence over what gets taught, since standards-based textbooks and tests define most curricula. Yet interest greatly influences learning, as it is a mixture of subject knowledge (Is the topic interesting?) and situational context (Is the task interesting?) (Deci and Ryan 1985). Therefore, understanding what topics and activities are of interest to your students can boost learning, and knowing what they're not interested in can be helpful as well. It's not a license, of course, to skip "the boring stuff," but it is a heads-up that you may need to pay more attention to the learning experiences designed around a particular topic.

Tenth-grade biology teacher Tiffany Glass has a good sense of the topics that most interest her students, but it doesn't mean that she takes it for granted. "Anything about sex and reproduction is always a winner with everyone," she shared. "But after that, it varies quite a bit." As a science educator, she is concerned with fostering more interest in the sciences among females and traditionally underrepresented students, and she sponsors an after-school science club. She also keeps up with research findings on this topic and read with interest the reported findings of the international Relevance of Science Education (ROSE) survey conducted with more than

Rate These Topics!

Directions: I am designing several mini-units for you to explore this year, but first I need some help. On a scale of 1–4, please rate your interest in these topics.

- 1: I'm there—sign me up!
- 2: This sounds interesting and I would possibly choose this.
- 3: Only if I have to.
- 4: Not a million years!

What are the causes and effects of eating disorders (anorexia, bulimia)?	1	2	3	4
What happens after something dies?	1	2	3	4
What are the effects of poisons on the body?	1	2	3	4
What are the advances in cancer treatment?	1	2	3	4
Why do some brain injuries result in behavior changes, while others don't?	1	2	3	4
What's the debate on stem cell research?	1	2	3	4
How do epidemics (black plague, bird flu) spread?	1	2	3	4
What contributes to the loss of endangered species?	1	2	3	4
How does war advance biotechnology?	1	2	3	4
What are the effects of radiation on the body?	1	2	3	4
How close are we to a vaccine for HIV/AIDS?	1	2	3	4
Why don't hereditary diseases like cystic fibrosis ever disappear?	1	2	3	4
How can organisms tolerate the hottest, coldest, wettest, and driest places on Earth?	1	2	3	4
Does everyone really have a twin?	1	2	3	4

Figure 3.10 *Interest survey in biology*

twelve hundred European adolescents (Elster 2007). The findings confirmed many observations she had made on her own through her years of teaching—namely, the girls in the study showed a higher interest in life sciences topics related to health (especially cancer, AIDS/HIV, and bulimia) while boys as a group were more interested in physical and technological science topics (especially atomic bombs and explosive chemicals) and had less interest in the life sciences overall.

Inspired by this study, Tiffany designed her own interest survey modeled on the ROSE instrument. She began with the standards document and her curricular materials and crafted statements for students to respond to (see Figure 3.10). She asked students in each of her periods to complete the survey anonymously. She used the results to design choice research activities throughout the year. For example, she had a strong response to the item "Why don't hereditary diseases like cystic fibrosis ever disappear?" and designed an activity that gave these students an opportunity to apply what they had learned about the Hardy-Weinberg principle of population equilibrium to the study of recessive mutation. "Finding out about their interests inspired me to get creative about my teaching," she told us. "This has been a great way to witness the ways to use what they're learning in meaningful ways."

■ Conclusion

As we have noted, background knowledge is linked with student achievement. It's a major contributor to student understanding and reading comprehension. Naturally, students have different sets of background knowledge based on their previous schooling and life experiences. The first step in developing and activating background knowledge is assessment. Teachers must first assess the content to determine which knowledge is core and which is incidental. From there, teachers must determine the knowledge their students already have—and the gaps in their current content knowledge. We've provided a number of tools that you can use to uncover students' background knowledge including anticipation guides, opinionnaires, cloze assessments, and interest surveys. Armed with information about the demands of the content and what students already know, you'll be ready to focus on activating the knowledge students already have.

Activating What Students Know

Teaching That Unearths and Upends
Students' Understandings

BACKGROUND KNOWLEDGE SHOULD BE FRONT and center in every classroom interaction. Why is it, then, that students so often sleep on what they know?
Might it be that we teachers have to do a better job of awakening it?

In this chapter, we focus on a number of instructional routines that get
that knowledge up and at 'em. We refer to them as instructional routines,
rather than strategies, because we want to move the professional conversation toward clarifying what we *teachers* do, and why we do it, in our classrooms. The term *strategies*, by contrast, seems to keep us in an eddy of
pinning students' lack of progress on their lack of strategies.

Think about what you know about the word *routine*. It's likely that
what comes to mind are the many nearly automatic behaviors you engage

in with little conscious thought. Picking up the newspaper off the front porch each morning, pouring milk in your coffee, locking the front door on the way out—these are all routines that have become ingrained. In the same way, we use instructional routines in our teaching to build habits among our students (Frey, Fisher, and Berkin 2008). These habits must include the learner's ability to activate that background knowledge—useful and useable—to understand her world. Ultimately, none of us has the luxury of having someone follow us around telling us what we need to bring to the learning table. Therefore, teachers must use instructional routines that over time become the habits of a self-directed learner, such as establishing purpose, identifying what you know and what you want to know, listening and filling in gaps, and talking with others. Many of these will seem familiar, but we consider each of these through the lens of activating background knowledge.

■ Establishing Purpose

As we noted in Chapter 1, one of the keys to improving comprehension is to help students activate useful background knowledge. Naturally, all background knowledge is not equally useful for reading a specific text. One of the ways that readers activate useful background knowledge is through setting a purpose. There are a number of possible purposes readers have for reading, including

- for pleasure

- to find something out

- to figure out how to solve a problem or fix something

- to talk about it (retell) with someone else

- to find out what happens

- to study for a test

- to answer questions

These generic purposes do help readers think about what they are reading. But as Pichert and Anderson (1977) demonstrated, when the purpose is more specific, readers understand better. Using a piece of text about a house (see Figure 4.1), Pichert and Anderson told some readers to read as home-buyers, asked others to read as burglars, and gave a third group no purpose.

The two boys ran until they came to the driveway. "See, I told you today was good for skipping school," said Mark. "Mom is never home on Thursday," he added. Tall hedges hid the house from the road so the pair strolled across the finely landscaped yard. "I never knew your place was so big," said Pete. "Yeah, but it's nicer now than it used to be since Dad had the new stone siding put on and added the fireplace."

There were front and back doors and a side door which led to the garage which was empty except for three parked 10-speed bikes. They went in the side door, Mark explaining that it was always open in case his younger sisters got home earlier than their mother.

Pete wanted to see the house so Mark started with the living room. It, like the rest of the downstairs, was newly painted. Mark turned on the stereo, the noise of which worried Pete. "Don't worry, the nearest house is a quarter of a mile away," Mark shouted. Pete felt more comfortable observing that no houses could be seen in any direction beyond the huge yard.

The dining room, with all the china, silver and cut glass, was no place to play so the boys moved into the kitchen where they made sandwiches. Mark said they wouldn't go to the basement because it had been damp and musty ever since the new plumbing had been installed.

"This is where my Dad keeps his famous paintings and his coin collection," Mark said as they peered into the den. Mark bragged that he could get spending money whenever he needed it since he'd discovered that his Dad kept a lot in the desk drawer.

There were three upstairs bedrooms. Mark showed Pete his mother's closet, which was filled with furs and the locked box, which held her jewels. His sisters' room was uninteresting except for the color TV, which Mark carried to his room. Mark bragged that the bathroom in the hall was his since one had been added to his sisters' room for their use. The big highlight in his room, though, was a leak in the ceiling where the old roof had finally rotted.

Figure 4.1 *"The House"*

Interestingly, these groups paid attention to different information within the text. In other words, the purpose directed them to attend to specific types of information, information that would be useful to their assigned roles. Importantly, the homebuyers and burglars both comprehended the text better than the group without a clear purpose.

Setting Purpose in U.S. History

In their U.S. history class, groups of students were reading different pieces of text about Japanese internment camps. Thomas Jenkins set a general purpose for reading, which was "to educate [themselves] so that [they could] analyze and interpret the U.S. government internment policy during World War II." On each piece of reading material, Thomas had written a question. The students in his class knew that the questions would guide their reading and that there was no clear-cut answer to each question that could be found in the text. For example, one group read "In Response to Executive Order 9066," by Dwight Okita (1983) (see Figure 4.2), on which the following question had been written: "What would it feel like to have neighbors and friends from school suddenly disappear because of their race?"

IN RESPONSE TO EXECUTIVE ORDER 9066:
ALL AMERICANS OF JAPANESE DESCENT MUST REPORT TO RELOCATION CENTERS

Dear Sirs:
Of course I'll come. I've packed my galoshes
and three packets of tomato seeds. Janet calls them
"love apples," My father says where we're going
they won't grow.

I am a fourteen-year-old girl with bad spelling
and a messy room. If it helps any, I will tell you
I have always felt funny using chopsticks
and my favorite food is pizza.
My best friend is a white girl named Denise—
we look at boys together. She sat in front of me
all through grade school because of our names:
O'Connor, Ozawa. I know the back of Denise's head very well.
I tell her she's going bald. She tells me I copy on tests.
We're best friends.

I saw Denise today in Geography class.
She was sitting on the other side of the room.
"You're trying to start a war," she said, "giving secrets away
to the Enemy. Why can't you keep your big mouth shut?"
I didn't know what to say.
I gave her a packet of tomato seeds
and asked her to plant them for me, told her
when the first tomato ripens,
to miss me.

Figure 4.2 *"In Response to Executive Order 9066"*

As this group of students negotiated their purpose and talked about the text, one girl, Kiki, recalled a previous lesson on *Nisei* (American-born Japanese) and *Issei* (Japanese immigrants) who were sent to the camps. "The girl in this poem is probably Nisei," she said. "This is the only country she has ever known, and it must feel so strange to her to be sent away." She read aloud the line "I have always felt funny using chopsticks and my favorite food is pizza" (Okita 1983, 211).

Roberto chuckled and said, "Me, too!"

"Her parents might be farmers, too, since she's got tomato seeds. Lots of Japanese people that got shipped to internment camps were farmers," offered Jacqueline.

"Let's look again at the question Thomas wrote," Miguel remarked. "It'd be bizarre to come to school one day and find a bunch of kids missing."

"Remember last year when our school did Every Fifteen Minutes, the drunken driving program? It was freaky when kids we knew started disappearing. That Grim Reaper guy would just come into a class and walk someone out. The next time you saw them, they were like a ghost. They wouldn't talk to you or nothing," Angel offered.

"Yeah, but it was like they were still there. Gone but not forgotten," Kiki said.

Roberto continued the conversation. "They got picked because they were part of the program, but what if it was just white kids, or all the black kids, or something messed up like that? What if the principal read an announcement like this that said you all gotta pack up and go today, and we don't know when you're coming back?"

"It's like when 9/11 happened, and some people had this stupid idea that we should do the same thing with anyone who was Muslim," reminded Angel. "My brother's been in the army since 2002 and he was telling me about that."

Miguel quickly responded, "Yeah, and if you think about it, we've done it before in America. Like with all the Native American tribes that got sent to reservations. Who was it that had to march, like, all the way across the country? You know, Trail of Tears?"

"Cherokee," Kiki replied. "They were living in Georgia and they were forced to go to Oklahoma."

"Not even Oklahoma," Roberto reminded the group. "There was *nothing* where they had to go."

"And you know they left friends and neighbors behind," Angel said. "One day they're there, and the next day they're not. That's messed up."

The group continued to discuss the poem and they wrote a reply to Mr. Jenkins' purpose-setting question. During this short conversation, the students used background knowledge learned from lessons early in the year as well as from this unit. In addition, they used prior shared experiences and information acquired from personal experiences. Their wide-ranging discussion moved from text-level interpretations to wider historical connections, and the question posed by their teacher focused the group on the task.

KWL (and Its Many Modifications)

The KWL instructional routine is well known among content area teachers as an effective way to activate background knowledge and cause students to link it to new information. In its classic form (Ogle 1986), the teacher leads a discussion and summarizes it on a three-column chart labeled "What I Know," "What I Want to Know," and "What I Learned."

KWL was conceived as a way to engage students in active reading by causing them to focus on what is known and not yet known. This hearty routine works well in so many content areas in part because it mirrors aspects of the scientific process. The K phase allows us to rapidly assess background knowledge; the W phase focuses students' attention on what can be learned based on the specific text when they make a plan for reading, reevaluate their questions, and activate background knowledge helpful in making meaning; and the L phase provides an opportunity for consolidating understanding in light of the text and the purpose for reading in the first place.

Educators and researchers have devised several adaptations of the original KWL format to further refine it, including

- *KWLH* (Ogle 1986): How can I learn more?

- *KWL Plus* (Carr and Ogle 1987): Adds mapping to the process

- *KWHLS* (Reid, Forrestal, and Cook 1989): How will I learn it? How will I share it?

- *KWLS* (Moore, Alvermann, and Hinchman 2000): What do I still need to learn?

- *KWHHL* (Szabo 2006): What are the head words? What are the heart words?

Each of these variations fosters metacognition by focusing the learner's attention on an aspect of learning, including creating a visual representation, collaborating with peers, planning future learning, and noticing vocabulary and tone. The selection of a particular variant of KWL should be guided by your teaching purpose. When we want our students to concentrate on their background knowledge, we insert a column of our own. KHWL invites students to list not only what they know but how they know it. This is quite challenging for students, who are not accustomed to naming their sources. However, formal academic discourse requires that learners are able to support their claims with evidence.

Eleventh-grade English teacher Maribelle Martine builds her course around rhetorical reading and writing because she knows this is critical for college success. Throughout the year, her students explore formal argumentation as a means for analyzing expository texts. She introduces Toulmin's (1958) elements of argument—claim, data, warrant, backing, qualifier, and rebuttal—as the touchstone for examining rhetoric and framing their writing

Element	Definition	Example
Claim	The assertion one intends to establish	*I have the right to hold and use the TV remote control as I see fit.*
Qualification	Setting the limitations for the claim	*When a parent or grandparent is in the room, he has the right of possession of the remote control.*
Data	Sources and facts that support the claim	*I consider the opinions of others in the room before I change the channel.* *I have never lost the remote control.*
Warrant	The way in which the data and the claim are connected	*My track record of courtesy and responsibility supports my claim that I should have the right to the remote control.*
Backing	Cultural beliefs and historical traditions that further support the claim	*There is a tradition of granting more responsibility and privilege to the oldest child.*
Rebuttal	The circumstances under which the claim would not be true or right	*When I am not watching TV, I do not have the right to possess the remote control.*

Figure 4.3 *Toulmin's elements of argument*

(see Figure 4.3). However, Maribelle also understands that rhetorical thought is not easily learned and demands many experiences before students will begin to internalize it. She is also aware that formal argument requires a tremendous amount of schema building and that learners typically learn major concepts in a stutter-step manner, with partial understandings gradually morphing into deeper and more complete knowledge (Wagner 2003).

Since a focus of her lesson today is on being able to name sources of knowledge, Maribelle has constructed a KHWL chart in order to draw their attention to how they know something. The class will read and discuss the transcript of a recent local city council debate on whether park entrance fees should be raised to cover rising expenses. Before they read, she wants to activate their background knowledge so that they can anticipate the claims on both sides of the argument. After introducing the topic, she asks them to reflect on what they know and how they know it.

"I'll start," Beatriz offers. "Everything is costing more. Food, gasoline, rent prices. They're all going up. The city's costs must be going up, too."

"And how do you know that? What's your data?" Maribelle asks.

"I heard my parents talking about it. It cost my mom sixty dollars to fill up the car yesterday, and she said that three years ago it only cost her twenty-five dollars."

"Other data sources that would support Beatriz?" Maribelle asks the class.

"Yeah, definitely. You could look at the city's budget to see how much they are spending on gasoline this year and last year to compare," replies Chris.

"OK, I see where you're going," Maribelle answers as she records their ideas on the chart. "What about an opposing argument?"

"That's easy," Adam remarks. "With everyone's cost of living going up, it's harder than ever to afford cheap entertainment. The city needs to hold park fees down so people can go."

"It's a good claim, but I want you to think about your data. How can you support this? This one's harder. Talk with each other," the teacher suggests.

The students confer with each other for a few minutes, and one student goes to a computer to find information. "Look at this," Lena says to her group members. "I learned about this in my consumer sciences class. The government has a cost-of-living index that reports on how prices change, like for food and energy. That would be a good data source."

The class continues its discussion for several minutes before diving into the city council transcripts. Maribelle is pleased with the results because she sees evidence that her students are becoming more practiced at linking their background knowledge to data, an essential skill for rhetorical writing.

Text Impression

The students in Lopresha Geene's eighth-grade social studies class were investigating people who made a difference before and during the Civil War. To activate their background knowledge, Lopresha provided her students with a list of words and asked them to create a piece of text using all of the words in order. As part of the introduction to this task, Lopresha said, "Let's get thinking about Harriet Tubman, the conductor of the Underground Railroad." Figure 4.4 contains the list of words in the left column and one student's response in the right column. Once they had finished, she read them a biographical entry from *Lives of Extraordinary Women: Rulers, Rebels (and*

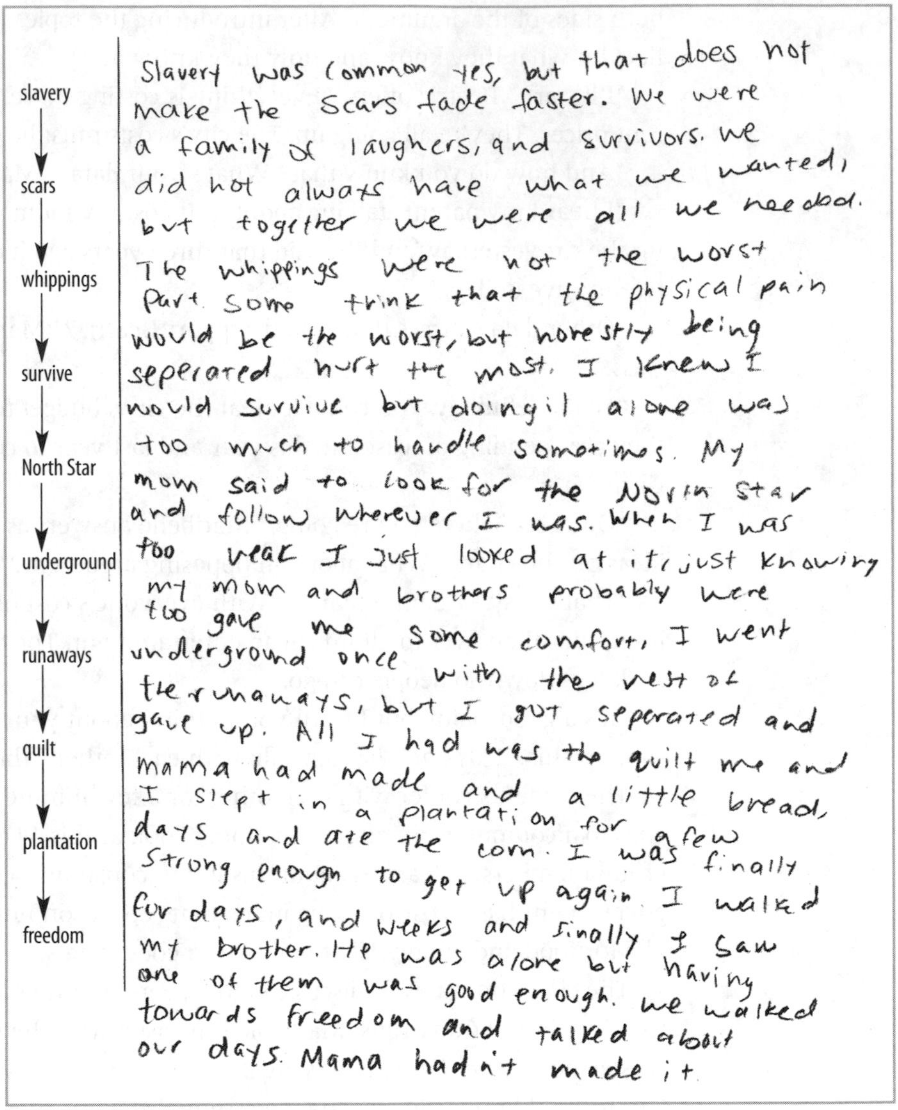

slavery → scars → whippings → survive → North Star → underground → runaways → quilt → plantation → freedom

Slavery was common yes, but that does not make the scars fade faster. We were a family of laughers, and survivors. we did not always have what we wanted, but together we were all we needed. The whippings were not the worst part. Some think that the physical pain would be the worst, but honestly being seperated hurt the most. I knew I would survive but doing it alone was too much to handle sometimes. My mom said to look for the North Star and follow wherever I was. When I was too weak I just looked at it, just knowing my mom and brothers probably were too gave me some comfort. I went underground once with the rest of the runaways, but I got seperated and gave up. All I had was the quilt me and mama had made and a little bread. I slept in a plantation for a few days and ate the corn. I was finally strong enough to get up again. I walked for days, and weeks and finally I saw my brother. He was alone but having one of them was good enough. we walked towards freedom and talked about our days. Mama hadn't made it.

Figure 4.4 *Text impression*

What the Neighbors Thought) (Krull 2000). The first paragraph of the text reads:

> "I think slavery is the next thing to hell," Harriet Tubman said. Her parents had been taken from the Ashanti tribe, warriors of West Africa, and brought to America as slaves; they had eleven children. At age five Harriet was put to work as a housekeeper and baby-sitter, and she grew up in fear. The scars on her back from many whippings were permanent, as was the brain damage after a two-pound lead weight was thrown at her head. (49)

The writing that Blake did, using the given words, primed her for understanding the text her teacher read to her. Originally called story impressions (McGinley and Denner 1987) and used with narrative texts, text impressions can be used with both narrative and informational texts. Blake's writing is reflective of her background knowledge about slavery, especially her understanding that the North Star was used as a guide for finding a northern passage to freedom. Other sentences reveal a partial understanding, such as "I went underground once with the rest of the runaways, but I got seperated [*sic*] and gave up." It is possible that she was not aware of the Underground Railroad, which would be a key part of Ms. Greene's unit. However, Blake's writing does reveal a core understanding of the nature of history, namely, that it is the story of human experience. Her text impression demonstrates the narrative sweep that compelling historical accounts contain, such as Tubman's biography written by Sarah Bradford in 1869. Lopresha planned to also share excerpts from Catherine Clinton's 2005 authoritative biography and compare and contrast the information. The class would also analyze the 1849 runaway slave ad posted in the *Cambridge Democrat* (see Figure 4.5). What began as an activation of background knowledge would later expand into fleshing out that knowledge more completely.

Quick Writes   One of easiest ways for teachers to activate students' background knowledge is through quick writes. Writers can't help but think while they write. By crafting a thought-provoking question and then asking them to write a brief (one- to five-minute) response, teachers help students notice what they know about a topic as well as what they don't know. Quick writes, when implemented properly, also provide a psychologically safe environment that gives students space to explore what they believe they know about a topic. In an interview with the ezine *Critique*, Peter Elbow, a leading voice in writing instruction, argues

> Writing feels inherently like a high stakes activity because you're putting it down in black and white. It's graded. It's for the teacher. Most people feel as though writing is high stakes and speaking is low stakes. But actually, writing is ideal for the low stakes use of words, for exploring, for taking chances, for trying to talk about something that other people might disagree with or disapprove of. Writing allows us to write something and not show it to anybody. In speaking, we're almost always speaking to somebody—and once you say something, you can never take it back. In our culture, we tend to use writing in high stakes ways and speaking in low stakes ways. But if we look at the actual technology of writing, writing is ideal for low stakes: you can look at it, throw it away, try it out, delete the file. (Bush n.d.)

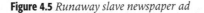

THREE HUNDRED DOLLARS REWARD.

RANAWAY from the subscriber on Monday the 17th ult., three negroes, named as follows: HARRY, aged about 19 years, has on one side of his neck a wen, just under the ear, he is of a dark chestnut color, about 5 feet 8 or 9 inches hight ; BEN, aged aged about 25 years, is very quick to speak when spoken to, he is of a chestnut color, about six feet high : MINTY, aged about 27 years, is of a chestnut color, fine looking, and about 5 feet high. One hundred dollars reward will be given for each of the above named negroes, if taken out of the State, and $50 each if taken in the State. They must be lodged in Baltimore, Easton or Cambridge Jail, in Maryland.

ELIZA ANN BRODESS.
Near Bucktown, Dorchester county, Md.
Oct. 3d, 1849.

☞The Delaware Gazette will please copy the above three weeks, and charge this office.

Figure 4.5 *Runaway slave newspaper ad*

Depending on the wording of the question, a teacher can use a quick write to tap into a student's background knowledge as it relates to declarative, procedural, or conditional knowledge (Fisher and Frey 2008). Declarative, procedural, and conditional knowledge are useful for illustrating how learning is applied in increasingly complex ways (Paris, Cross, and Lipson 1984; see Figure 4.6). For quick-write prompts, choose questions that activate the proper type of knowledge you are seeking from your students. As an example, consider the conditional, procedural, and declarative knowledge related to making an inference as outlined in Figure 4.7.

During a unit of study on the human nervous system, students in Barbara Harris' biology class write daily. She knows that this content is challenging for many students and that she must regularly activate their background knowledge so that students make connections with new information. She

Type of Knowledge	What It Is	Example
Declarative	Facts, labels, names	What are the common types of reading comprehension instruction?
Procedural	Application of information	How does a reader use these to support his reading comprehension?
Conditional	Knowing when and why to apply information	In what ways can these reading comprehension instructional routines be implemented in your classroom?

Figure 4.6 *Types of knowledge*

Conditional	Procedural	Declarative
I know . . . • when to do this • why I am doing this	I know . . . • how to do this • the process and the procedures to use	I know . . . • what this means
	Example	
I know . . . • I must infer when the author fails to reveal things explicitly. I do this because the author is expecting me, as the reader, to fill in the gaps she has left in the text. I realize the difference between implicit and explicit.	I know . . . • when I read, I need to think about my prior knowledge and experiences about something similar. For example, when I read about a character who entered a deserted house on a dark and stormy night, I know from my experience the character is likely feeling uneasy because of my own experience about dark nights and empty houses.	I know . . . • that an inference is combining information from my knowledge and experience with what is in the text.

Figure 4.7 *Conditional, procedural, and declarative knowledge relate to making inferences*

also knows that this is one area of science in which students have a number of misconceptions that she must address. To ensure that their background knowledge is activated and misconceptions are addressed, Barbara starts each class with a quick write. This unit includes the following prompts:

- You might have heard the statement "Humans use only 10 percent of their brains." Summarize the evidence either for or against this claim.

Melissa

⊕ Not feeling pain can be painful. In other words feeling it can hurt, but not feeling it can be harmful. Pain is an alarm, it lets you know when your body is not functioning correctly. Not feeling pain can be an asset as well.

⊕ Not feeling pain can be undesirrable. For example you are in the situation where you cannot feel any pain. Your wearing a long-sleeve shirt and you realize it is on fire. You look at your hand and its completly melted, and burnt off your arm. The whole time your hand was on the stove burning, but you didn't feel it because you could not feel any pain.

⊕ Pain is like an alarm. It is an exotic feeling that the body feels and sends a message to the

Figure 4.8 *Melissa's quick write on pain*

- The human cerebrum is disproportionately large compared with the cerebrum of other animals. What advantage does this give to humans?

- Hypothesize why it takes more energy for a nerve impulse to travel through an axon that lacks myelin as opposed to an axon that has myelin.

- A rare condition exists in which a person cannot feel pain. Is this desirable or undesirable? Explain your response.

Melissa's response to the last prompt is shown in Figure 4.8. Her background knowledge about this topic is obvious in her writing. She understands that pain has a protective quality and that both the brain and nerves work together to transmit the pain message and trigger a protective response ("The brain responds to the message and lets the body know to move away, or that something is wrong."). She relates this concept to one that is more familiar ("Pain is like an alarm.")—evidence that she is

brain. The brain responds to the message and lets the body know to move away, or that something is wrong.

Some people might say not feeling pain when it is taking place in your body, can be desireable. For example you are going to be in a triatholon in two months. You start working and you don't feel any pain from your muscles being worked. But then again, you can damage and tear your muscles by not stopping.

Figure 4.8 *Continued*

activating other schemata. She also uses personal experience to foreground her understanding. Melissa is an athlete who follows a fitness regime most would find difficult. In the last paragraph, she explains, "For example, you are going to be in a triatholon [*sic*] in two months. You start working and you don't feel any pain from your muscles being worked. But then again, you can damage and tear your muscles by not stopping." You can almost hear the conversation going on in her head as she contemplates the pros and cons of not feeling pain. By engaging in low-stakes writing, she is able to activate her background knowledge and consider how multiple schemata interface.

Structured Partner Discussions

Middle and high school teachers commonly begin instruction with brief partner discussions because they prepare the group for the lesson and motivate students through engagement with the topic. When questioned, teachers will tell us that they do this to activate background knowledge, but our observation is that these discussions are more often unstructured, with little or no teacher follow-up to ascertain whether the information shared was correct or valuable. These situations might provide students some relevance to the content, but they often do not activate background knowledge. This can be mitigated somewhat by asking for responses from the whole class, but again, these are usually cursory, and after two or three answers, the teacher moves on.

It seems to us that if we are to activate background knowledge then we also have an obligation to follow up in order to make sure it is accurate and useful. Otherwise, these peer-led conversations can reinforce misconceptions or take learners off topic. This poses a dilemma, because checking in on all those conversations can fill an entire period, and then there's no time left to engage with the new information.

A fishbowl technique allows for following up on partner discussions (White 1974). After inviting partner discussion on a topic, ask several pairs of students to repeat their discussion in front of the class. Don Bainbridge uses this approach in his sixth-grade mathematics classroom to get his students thinking about their problem-solving approaches. "I start the lesson off with a problem I've posted on the board. I don't want them to solve it, but I do want them to talk about what they will do to solve it. They know I'm going to pick a few pairs to talk about their discussion, and I let each group know in advance. They call themselves guppies because they know we're going to fishbowl," he said. "I even have a sign hanging from a light fixture that says, 'Math Fishbowl.' It's become a daily routine in my class, and it lets me fix any problems or misconceptions before we proceed further." Fishbowls can also be used to provide students with a peer model and demonstration, as an in-process tool to help refine and enhance peer-to-peer interaction and discussion, and as a debriefing technique to consolidate what was learned (Schmuck and Runkel 1985).

Physical education teacher and football coach Randy Jankowski uses a whip-around instructional routine to check on students' background knowledge. "Every year during training camp I assign a book for the whole team to read," he explained. "Like last year, we read *Friday Night Lights* [Bissinger 2000]. This summer we're going read *Gym Candy* [Deuker 2007]. It's a novel, but it brings up a lot of serious issues about steroid use in high school football."

Older members of the team know that the coach has a book for them every year, so they're not surprised when he introduces *Gym Candy* to them. "Now, you can tell from the title it's about steroids. I know you're all feeling the pressure to make the cut, to perform. And there's that temptation to load up a little. Get bigger, get faster, and get stronger. But there's a dark side, too. I'd like for you to take a few minutes to make a list of the things you know about steroids. Then we'll do a whip-around," Coach Jankowski commands. The boys are familiar with the process of listing what they know on paper, then standing. Each member of the team reads one item on his list, and the others cross off facts as they are stated. They return to their seats when every item on their list has been shared (Fisher and Frey 2007). This being a competitive group, the last one standing gets to run five fewer laps.

After several minutes of reflection and writing, the group is ready. In short order, players share the following facts:

- Anabolic steroids contain testosterone.

- Steroids can be detected with a blood test.

- They build up muscles.

- It's illegal to use them if you are a minor.

- You can get bad zits from taking steroids.

- You need a prescription from a doctor to take them.

- You can get them in Mexico.

- Steroids are dangerous for girls because then you look like a dude.

- Steroids can be either pills or shots.

- They can cause cancer.

Sean is the last player standing, and he's quite happy that he'll have fewer laps to complete today. Coach Jankowski is pleased with the overall level of background knowledge and satisfied that they have a suitable level to begin the book. "Course, knowing something and *understanding* it are two different things," Coach remarks. "That's why I picked this book as a good way to get the conversation going about tough choices."

For those teachers who are exploring new technologies in their classrooms, the "clicker" revolution is an exciting one. These student response systems allow learners to answer questions posed by their teacher and see the results graphed immediately. Students use a small device about the size of a remote control to select an answer to a multiple-choice question. The questions can be embedded into a PowerPoint presentation for ease of use. Educators are using this process to check students' understanding throughout their lessons. Eric Mazur, physics professor at Harvard, has been a leading proponent in this work. He has constructed items he calls ConcepTests, which are really short scenarios related to physics principles, and poses these to his students every fifteen minutes or so (Duncan and Mazur 2005). For example, "A rubber bullet and an aluminum bullet, equal in size and mass, are fired at a block of wood at the same speed. The rubber bullet bounces back, while the aluminum one penetrates. Which is more likely to knock the block over?" (Koman 1995). After selecting their answer, students see the correct answer (the rubber bullet is more likely to knock over the wood block) and view a bar graph of how their classmates did.

Teachers can use clicker technology to check whether the background knowledge they have activated is correct, by combining it with the partner talk processes commonly used in the classroom. Consider the question Russell Bernstein asked of his seventh-grade life science students at the beginning of a lesson: "True or false: Muscle turns to fat if you stop exercising." Students began to quickly buzz in with their choices, and then Mr. Bernstein projected the class results (61 percent answered true, while 39 percent answered false), but not the correct answer.

"We've got quite a disagreement going here. Before I tell you the answer, I would like for you to talk to the person sitting to your left. Each of you explain why you chose your answer," he directed. After a few minutes, he spoke to them again. "Now do the same thing with the person on your right. This time, I want you to talk about what you think is the correct answer, even if it's different from your original choice."

After the second round of partner talks, he regained their attention. "You've had a chance to answer the question and then discuss it with two of your classmates. Now, let's answer the question again." With that, he projected the question again, and this time the results changed quite a bit. Only 18 percent of the students answered true, while the majority (82 percent) chose false. Russell asked them why they had changed their answers.

Bret replied, "When I talked to Rachel, she told me it couldn't happen because they are two different kinds of cells."

Maria offered, "Jamie said she picked false because her mom told her that it might seem that way, but it's really that your muscles get smaller and your fat gets more. That made sense to me."

By checking the accuracy of their background knowledge and then allowing them to talk with one another about their reasoning, Russell was able to affect a change regarding this commonly held misconception. He also knew that nearly 20 percent of the class still did not understand this point, so he would need to continue to build their core knowledge of cell structures.

Checklists
As we have noted, sometimes students have the necessary knowledge in their brains but, for some reason, fail to activate that knowledge. There are a number of reasons for this, "sins" of memory, as Schacter (1999) called them, but our job is to make sure that memories are activated.

One of the ways to activate background knowledge and keep it activated throughout a task completion is through the systematic use of checklists. This may seem obvious, as most of us use checklists in our daily lives. Some people can't even visit a grocery store without their shopping list. The list serves as a reminder and keeps information front and center.

Checklists for academic tasks do the same thing. Strickland and Strickland (2000), for example, note that checklists can serve to remind students of specific behaviors or abilities they should display while completing a task. Gere, Christenbery, and Sassi (2005) note that checklists can serve to keep learners on task, which we recognize is important for memory creation and retrieval. However, our experience with checklists suggests that they are powerful tools for activating background knowledge. Armed with a checklist in hand, students are systematically confronted with the knowledge they need to be successful.

Mariana Ramirez gave her ninth-grade students a checklist borrowed from a list developed by Rowlands (2007). The terms on the checklist were not new to them. By the time they reach high school, students have heard *purpose*, *audience*, *content*, and *organization* throughout their schooling experiences. But Mariana knows that students often fail to remember about these components of quality writing—that is, activate their background knowledge. Using a checklist that identifies core information required of writers (see Figure 4.9), Mariana was able to reinforce their background knowledge about considerations when composing original text, while also conceptually chunking to help them move beyond following a sequence of steps. This approach is consistent with the effectiveness of establishing subgoals to foster transfer of skills, discussed in Chapter 1 (Atkinson, Catrambone, and Merrill 2003).

Algebra teacher Lisa Hartson also uses a checklist with her students. She knows that her students have the knowledge necessary to solve word problems but worries that they get stressed and fail to follow the steps they've been taught. The checklist Lisa created is based on the SQRQCQ framework developed by Fay (1965), which is based on the SQ3R (survey, question, read, recite, review) framework developed by Robinson (1961). As can be seen in Figure 4.10, the steps are clearly outlined for students. In addition, there is a reference in this checklist to another checklist that focuses on the signal words that indicate which operations are necessary. For example, word problems that ask for a *sum* or *total of* require addition, whereas *less than*, *decreased by*, and *difference of* require subtraction.

Checklists also allow teachers to assess where thinking went astray. Brian was confronted with the following word problem:

> A group of 266 persons consists of men, women, and children. There are four times as many men as children, and twice as many women as children. How many of each are there?

According to his checklist, Brian had surveyed the problem and asked the first question. However, he was stuck in the rereading phase because he could not identify the information necessary to answer the question. This information allowed Lisa to guide this thinking.

Lisa: Let's look again at the information given in the problem. What do you know?

Brian: There are 266 people, but they are a mix of men, women, and children and I need to figure out how many of each.

Ask yourself . . .

❑ *Purpose*: Have you defined the purpose of your writing? Are you trying to entertain? Explain? Describe? Analyze? Define? Persuade? Something else? Are the content and the tone of your piece appropriate for your purpose? _____

❑ *Audience*: Have you identified your intended reader(s)? Have you thought about the content of your piece (examples, details, quoted materials) in terms of how the reader is likely to respond? _____

❑ *Content*: Have you reread each paragraph carefully, asking yourself, "What else does my reader need to know here?" and "Do I need to gather more information to fill in content gaps?"_____

❑ *Organization*: Is the organization of your piece as effective as possible? Do your examples build to the strongest at the end? Would it be more effective to begin your piece with your conclusion followed by support? Or would it be more effective to lead your readers through the story of your thinking so they will reach the conclusion the same way you did?_____

❑ *Introduction*: Is your introduction engaging? Should you begin with a quotation? A description? An anecdote? A shocking detail? Something else?_____

❑ *Conclusion*: Does your conclusion do more than simply repeat or summarize what you have already said? Does it leave the reader with a fresh understanding and/or something more to think about? _____

Figure 4.9 *Sample writing checklist*

_____ S (survey)	Skim to get the main idea of the problem.
_____ Q (question)	Find the question that is asked in the problem.
_____ R (read)	Read the problem and identify the information and details provided.
_____ Q (question)	Ask what operation needs to be performed (if necessary, see signal word checklist for operations).
_____ C (compute)	Solve the problem mathematically.
_____ Q (question)	Ask yourself, "Does the answer make sense?"

Figure 4.10 *SQRQCQ algebra checklist*

Lisa: Yes, exactly. You have the survey done. You also have the first question done. You know that the problem is to figure out how many of each. Let's reread this one carefully to see what hints we can find. [*They read the problem together.*]

Brian: So, there are four times the men as the children. But I don't know how many men there are. And then they tell me about how many women there are, but I don't know how many children there are.

Lisa: Exactly. And what do we do when we don't know a specific number?

Brian: We make that one *x*?

Lisa: Perfect! I think you're stuck there. You have to decide which one you want to make *x* and then set up the other variables. What will you let *x* equal—the number of men, women, or children?

Brian: I guess the kids because there are more men, four times.

Lisa: Good choice. I think you're ready to return to the checklist and work through the rest of the problem. I like the way you're using what you know to solve that problem. Keep at it.

Brian worked his way through the rest of the problem. At the last step of the checklist, he added up his answers for children (38), men (152), and women (76) to make sure that they added to a total of 266 people.

Sentence and Paragraph Frames

Sometimes students have a lot of information in their minds but don't know how to organize that information. Simply providing them with a sentence or paragraph frame can unlock the information students have in their heads. When students are provided this type of structure, the content follows. Think of it as a scaffold. The frames reduce some of the cognitive demand of the task while also provoking background knowledge. Dutro

(2005) noted that writing frames are especially effective with English language learners who often get tripped up with grammar and vocabulary despite the fact that they understand the information. For example, Dutro suggests the use of the following sentence frame to help students write a compare-and-contrast essay: _____ and _____ share several characteristics, including _____.

Shelene used this frame in her geography essay when she wrote:

> California and Florida share several characteristics,
> including oceans, oranges, and lots of tourism.

College composition experts Gerald Graff and Cathy Birkenstein (2006) recommend the use of frames (they call them templates) as an effective way for developing students' academic writing skills. In response to the criticism that templates result in formulaic writing, Graff and Birkenstein respond:

> After all, even the most creative forms of expression depend on established patterns and structures. Most songwriters, for instance, rely on a time-honored verse-chorus-verse pattern, and few people would call Shakespeare uncreative because he didn't invent the sonnet or dramatic forms that he used to such dazzling effect. . . . Ultimately, then, creativity and originality lie not in the avoidance of established forms, but in the imaginative use of them. (10–11)

We often use published authors as a source for writing frames. For example, we introduce writing frames using the poem "If I Were in Charge of the World," by Judith Viorst (1981). The first stanza of the poem reads:

> If I were in charge of the world
> I'd cancel oatmeal,
> Monday mornings,
> Allergy shots, and also Sara Steinberg. (1)

Edgar used this opportunity to tell us what was important to him when he wrote:

> If I were in charge of the world
> I'd cancel posers,
> police raids,
> country music,
> and also bras.

English teacher Heather Jacobs used writing frames in a unit on poetry. She shared the poem "Where I'm From," by George Ella Lyon (1999; see Figure 4.11), with her students. Together, the students and their teacher

I am from clothespins,
from Clorox and carbon-tetrachloride.
I am from the dirt under the back porch.
(Black, glistening
it tasted like beets.)
I am from the forsythia bush,
the Dutch elm
whose long gone limbs I remember
as if they were my own.
I'm from fudge and eyeglasses,
from Imogene and Alafair.
I'm from the know-it-alls
and the pass-it-ons,
from perk up and pipe down.
I'm from He restoreth my soul
with a cottonball lamb
and ten verses I can say myself.
I'm from Artemus and Billie's Branch,
fried corn and strong coffee.
From the finger my grandfather lost
to the auger
the eye my father shut to keep his sight.
Under my bed was a dress box
spilling old pictures,
a sift of lost faces
to drift beneath my dreams.
I am from those moments—
snapped before I budded—
leaf-fall from the family tree.

Figure 4.11 *"Where I'm From," by George Ella Lyon*

analyzed the structure of the poem and how the author constructed and
shared her ideas. This task required a great deal of background knowledge,
some of which was core and some of which was incidental. Heather was not
worried about the incidental background knowledge that her students
might not have, such as carbon-tetrachloride or specific types of plants. The
core knowledge that she wanted to activate and build centered on self-
disclosures. She knew that each of her students had personal experiences
that they wanted to share but did not know how to do so.

Using a paragraph frame (see Figure 4.12), Heather's students wrote their own versions of the "Where I'm From" poem. As you can see from Bobby's work (Figure 4.13), students had to draw on their personal experiences with the world and their knowledge about poems to complete the task. Bobby, whose given name is Timothy, lived in Hawaii before moving to San Diego in tenth grade. In addition to informing the teacher and providing an outlet for expression, these poems served as fodder for the biographical incidents that students would write later in the school year.

Once students are used to the "Where I'm From" frame, they can use it in content area classes as well. Kimberly chose this frame from a selection of possible frames to demonstrate her understanding of Chilean dictator Augusto Pinochet in her world history class. The writing frame provoked her understanding of Pinochet, as can be seen in Figure 4.14.

Frames can be used with informational text as well (Lewis and Wray 1995). Consider the discussion frame in Figure 4.15. Using this frame, students can summarize and synthesize information. The frame provides structure for the grammar and mechanics of writing while requiring students to use their background knowledge. These types of frames are especially useful as pre- and posttest assessments as they provide concrete evidence of students' thinking before and after a unit of study. Over time, and with exposure to a number of sentence and paragraph frames, students begin to incorporate them into their own speaking and writing. For example, Kimberly used the discussion frame in preparation for her final exam in world history to summarize her thinking about the use of propaganda leading up to World War I (see Figure 4.16, page 90). She applied her background knowledge of Stefan Zweig, the pacifist Austrian novelist and playwright, to support her assertion that "without even understanding the conditions of the war, people gave their support." She went on to contrast this with the opposing view that "propaganda is a completely legitimate way to promote patriotism." She finished her summary by stating, "Once people make an attempt to control another's actions, humanitarianism is lost."

Sentence and paragraph frames aid students in their writing, and in their thinking, because they reduce the linguistic demands of the task and allow students to use what they know. Kimberly obviously possessed a great deal of background knowledge from her work in world history, but the paragraph frame helped her formalize her thoughts. As such, frames are an excellent way to activate students' background knowledge about the content while also extending it to another level.

I am from _____ (specific ordinary item), from _____ (product name) and _____.

I am from the _____ (home description . . . adjective, adjective, sensory detail).

I am from the _____ (plant, flower, natural item), the _____ (plant, flower, natural detail).

I am from _____ (family tradition) and _____ (family trait), from _____ (name of family member) and _____ (another family name) and _____ (family name).

I am from the _____ (description of family tendency) and _____ (another one).

From _____ (something you were told as a child) and _____ (another).

I am from (representation of religion or lack of it). (Further description.)

I'm from _____ (place of birth and family ancestry), _____ (two food items representing your family).

From the _____ (specific family story about a specific person and detail), the _____ (another detail), and the _____ (another detail about another family member).

I am from _____ (location of family pictures, mementos, archives and several more lines indicating their worth).

Figure 4.12 *Paragraph frame for "Where I'm From"*

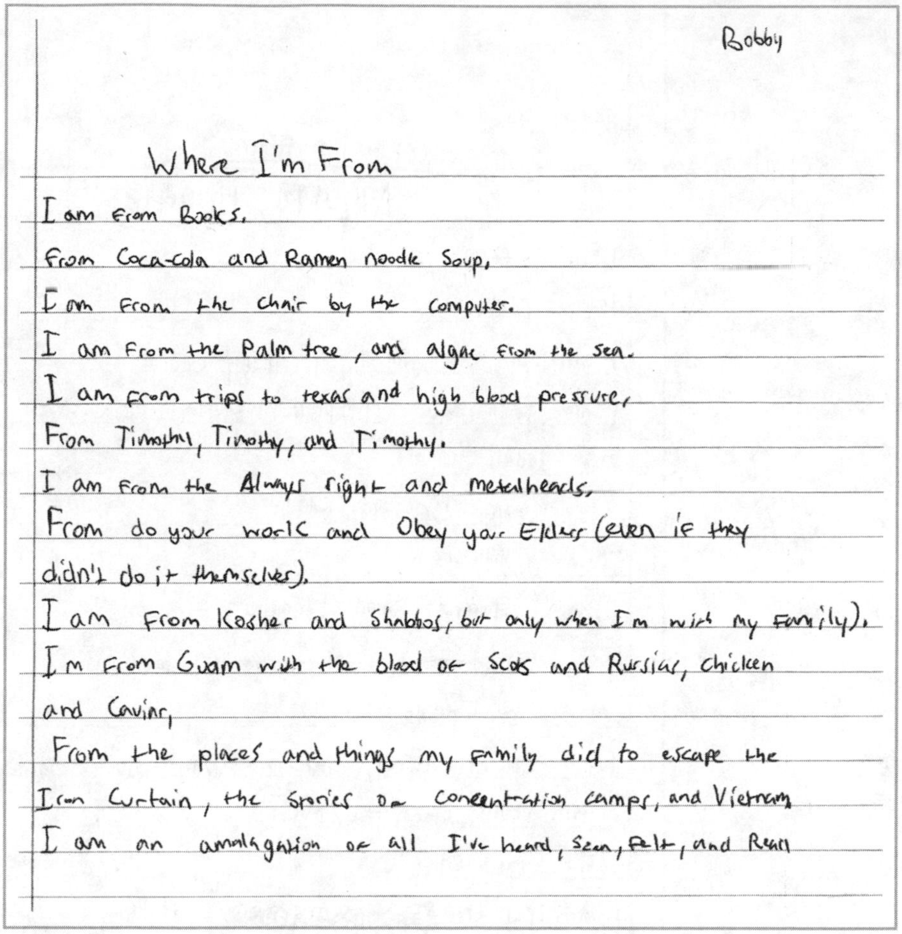
Bobby

Where I'm From

I am from Books.
From Coca-cola and Ramen noodle Soup,
I am From the chair by the computer.
I am From the Palm tree, and algae from the sea.
I am from trips to texas and high blood pressure,
From Timothy, Timothy, and Timothy.
I am from the Always right and metalheads,
From do your work and Obey your Elders (even if they
didn't do it themselves).
I am From Kosher and Shabbos, but only when I'm with my Family).
I'm From Guam with the blood of Scots and Russian, chicken
and Caviar,
From the places and things my family did to escape the
Iron Curtain, the stories on concentration camps, and Vietnam
I am an amalgation of all I've heard, Seen, Felt, and Read

Figure 4.13 *Student writing using "Where I'm From" frame*

Conclusion

Activating relevant background knowledge is a critical component of quality teaching. Importantly, it's not something that's done only at the outset of a unit or lesson. We're not talking about the anticipatory set or hook of the Madeline Hunter (1976) days or about making sure that students see the relevance in the curriculum. While those are important parts of lessons, they aren't enough to ensure students learn at high levels.

As the examples in this chapter suggest, the activation of background knowledge has to occur throughout teaching and learning. As we have

Where I'm From
AUGUSTO PINOCHET

I am from lemons

from molasses

I am from the soles of army boots

I am from the enormous weeping willow

the fallen acorns

I am from cock fights

and violence

from Pinochet and Martinez

I am from ~~the pride of capitalism~~ fascism

and blind pride

From sit and listen and do what you're told

I am from ~~crucifix~~ crucifixes

and crowded pews

I am from ~~Argentina Argentina~~ Chile,

farms and humidity

From the rise and fall of military power

the weaponry

and the murder of Salvador Allende

I am from September 1973

but no more, my time of supremacy has come to an end

Figure 4.14 *Student writing using "Where I'm From" frame*

There is a lot of discussion about whether _____ . The people who agree with this idea, such as _____ , claim that _____

_____

_____ . They also argue that _____

_____ . A further point they make is _____

_____

_____ .

However, there are also strong arguments against this point of view. _____ believe(s) that_____

_____

_____ .

Another counterargument is _____

_____

_____ .

Furthermore, _____

_____

_____ .

After looking at the different points of view and the evidence for them, I think _____ ,

because _____

_____

_____ .

Figure 4.15 *Discussion frame*

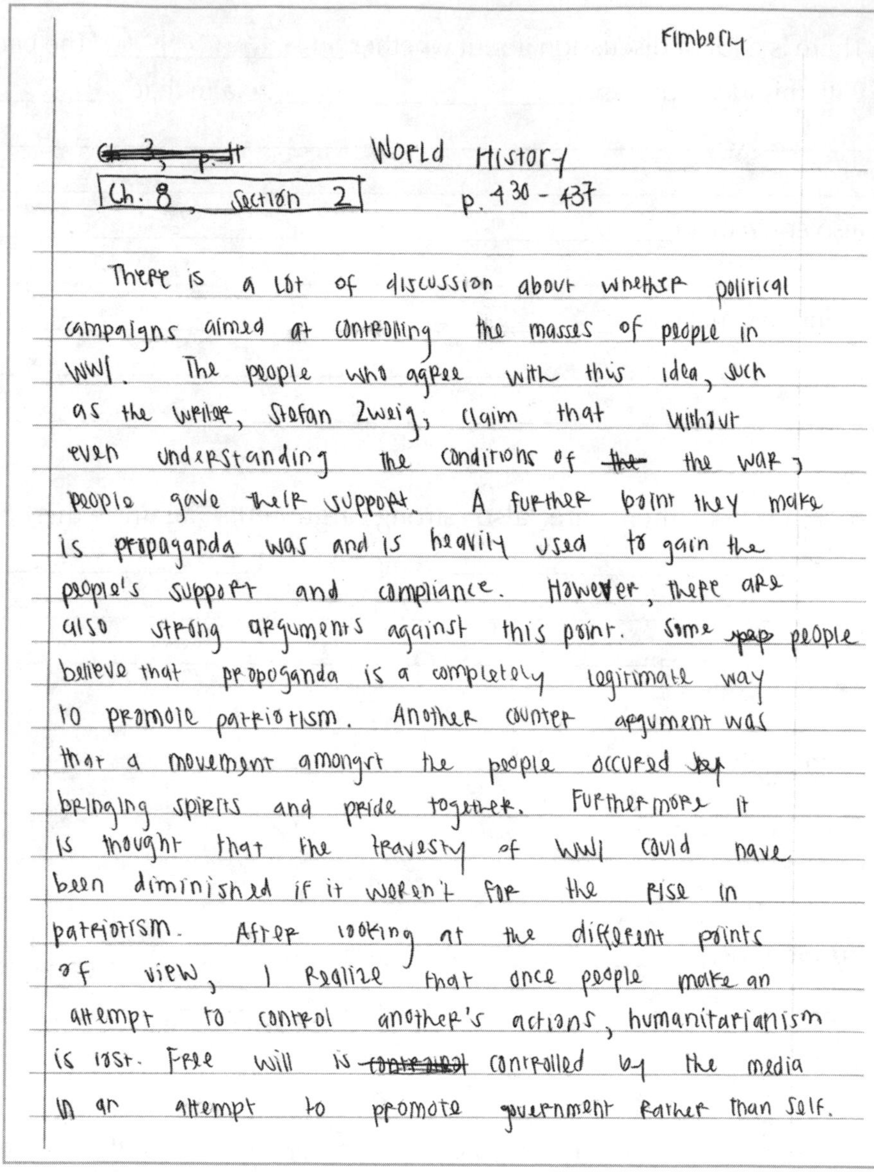

World History

Ch. 8, Section 2   p. 430 - 437

There is a lot of discussion about whether political campaigns aimed at controlling the masses of people in WWI. The people who agree with this idea, such as the writer, Stefan Zweig, claim that without even understanding the conditions of ~~the~~ the war, people gave their support. A further point they make is propaganda was and is heavily used to gain the people's support and compliance. However, there are also strong arguments against this point. Some ~~pep~~ people believe that propoganda is a completely legitimate way to promote patriotism. Another counter argument was that a movement amongst the people occured bringing spirits and pride together. Furthermore it is thought that the travesty of WWI could have been diminished if it weren't for the rise in patriotism. After looking at the different points of view, I realize that once people make an attempt to control another's actions, humanitarianism is lost. Free will is ~~controlled~~ controlled by the media in an attempt to promote government rather than self.

Figure 4.16 *Student writing using discussion frame*

noted before, background knowledge has to be at the heart of every classroom interaction. It's the only way we know how to ensure that students grow and develop. It's also the only way we know how to update the knowledge that learners have in their minds. By activating background knowledge, we allow new information to modify or validate understanding. And after all, that's the goal of schooling.

Quickening the Pace of Students' Background Knowledge Acquisition

"LIFE ISN'T EVEN-STEVEN," ONE OF OUR GRANDPARENTS used to say. And it isn't. The world roils with inequities. We've taught children who by middle school have traveled the world, been to phenomenal summer camps, and soaked up the "world is your oyster" attitude and advantages of affluent, educated parents. On the other hand, we've taught children from poverty who have literally never traveled out of their towns and often lagged behind on the background knowledge that counts in America. We've also taught children who grew up outside of the United States and as immigrants had rich background experiences that were different from other students in the class. Some of our students have had little exposure to books, museums, the Internet. If you peeked in their files, you might see that some of these children have IQs higher than some of the financially advantaged kids. And there's the rub: even the brightest child is going to suffer academically if he is not exposed to the knowledge that counts in our culture.

In this chapter, we take on a couple of hard questions: To what extent can we as teachers make up for these inequities? Can we catch up the kids who are behind? Our answer: Yes, we can. And we do this by adapting our teaching so that it more purposefully and intensely contributes to the experiential bases of our students. We can quicken the pace at which students assimilate new information. In short, we're not helpless and students are not hopeless.

We're reminded of a former student, Abdurashid. He grew up in Ethiopia but was forced to flee the country for political reasons. With the members of his family who survived the journey across the desert, he lived in a Kenyan refugee camp for five years. Eventually, some, but not all, of the family members were granted entrance into the United States. Abdurashid enrolled in our school. When he arrived, Abdurashid spoke several languages including Oromo, Amharic, and Somali, but not English. Naturally, he gained a great deal of world knowledge from his experiences but lacked school knowledge as the refugee camps did not provide any formal education. Part of our job, as his teachers, was to quickly build his background knowledge. He needed information about school as well as the myriad of references he would hear as a ninth grader in a Californian school. We fully understood that we could not compensate for all of his missing experiences, and we knew that we could draw on the experiences he'd had that our other students had not had. Our goal with Abdurashid was to ensure that he rapidly gained background knowledge that would serve him well in the four years he would attend our school.

There are more and less effective ways for doing this. For example, it is unlikely that round-robin reading, in which students are required to read texts aloud to the class, will improve students' understanding or build their background knowledge (Opitz and Rasinski 1998). Talking with elders about their experiences or visiting a museum, on the other hand, will probably build students' funds of knowledge (Gonzalez, Moll, and Amanti 2005). Funds of knowledge typically include "the intellectual and social knowledge existing in families and communities," according to the Center for Research on Education, Diversity and Excellence (crede.berkeley.edu /tools/glossary.html), so it's easy to see how elders and museums can build this knowledge.

But let's remember why we're doing this. We're focused on building background because it's critical to learning, and not because we think that all students need to have the same information in their heads. In fact, we take exception to the idea that there are specific topics that are critical in specific grade levels, as E. D. Hirsch asserts, because it sets up a doom scenario for students like Abdurashid. It perpetuates the idea that there is no way to catch up if you try to amass knowledge later in life. And we question the Euro-centeredness of the knowledge base that tends to get privileged by this grade-specific stance on knowledge acquisition. As Abdurashid, who is currently a premed student at a well-known university, taught us, background knowledge is cumulative and can be built and activated by skilled teachers. And as Marshall reminds us, "learning is controlled as much by experiences students bring to the learning situation as it is by the way the information is presented" (1996, 81).

■ The Learning Cycle

A great deal of time and attention has gone into understanding learning from behavioral and neurological perspectives (e.g., Howard 2006; Schunk 2007). As we discussed in Chapter 1, learning focuses on modifying what is already known. In essence, learning validates or modifies schemata (Anderson 1977). As Piaget (1985) noted, there is a biological drive for learners to reach a balance between their cognitive structures and their environment. He called this drive *equilibration* and noted that it involved both of his other constructs, assimilation and accommodation. Piaget believed that learners attempt to make sense of the world around them by assimilating new information into their existing mental schemes and accommodating, or changing, these schemes as necessary (Duncan 1995).

These constructs are noteworthy in relation to building background knowledge as well. Assimilation allows the learner to integrate new information into an existing schema. For example, Jessica has a general schema for marine animals and can add information from a newspaper article about a shark attack into her existing knowledge. Accommodation requires that the learner revise, restructure, or alter her schema to account for new information. When Jessica is confronted with the claim that shark attacks are increasing because of climate changes and food supplies, she has to accommodate this new information because she wasn't previously aware that sharks are being affected by increased temperatures. You can hear her accommodation as she asks questions:

Jessica:	He says that the sharks are attacking because of climate change. I thought that was about the temperature on Earth going up and there being more seawater.
Erik Jackson:	It is. But I think the author is trying to inform you that the increasing temperature is impacting the ocean and food supplies.
Jessica:	But global warming is caused by more CO_2, right? It doesn't make sense that sharks would have less food because of the air.
Erik:	I think it's a worthy question to research. What exactly is the food cycle for a shark? I don't know, but I think the author thinks that somewhere along the way climate change is impacting the food supply.
Jessica:	Maybe. But I don't know. Global warming and climate change are about the same thing. I get that there will probably be more seawater when icebergs melt. But there is still the same amount of food.

Let's leave Jessica and her struggle to reestablish equilibration and look at learning in general. We define learning as change. And this change, or learning, occurs as a cycle, not in discrete chunks. Figure 5.1 provides a graphic representation of the learning cycle adapted from Marshall (1996).

Theoretically, you can start anywhere in the cycle to create learning. Many teachers start by providing students information in the hope of creating understanding, which in turn modifies prior (background) knowledge.

But our experience and evaluation of the research (e.g., Alvermann 2001; Dochy, Segers, and Buehl 1999; Strangman and Hall 2004) suggest that teachers should start with background knowledge. As shown graphically in Figure 5.1, background knowledge generates purpose. And there is considerable evidence that purpose is a critical variable in student learning (Hill and Flynn 2006; Torrance 2007). As discussed in Chapter 4, when students understand the purpose of the lesson, they know where to direct their attention and how to focus on the task at hand.

Continuing with the learning cycle, attention encourages the learner to seek out and select information. This is where inquiry and motivation enter the equation. When the learner has a purpose or desire to know something, he will seek information from texts, peers, the teacher, and a

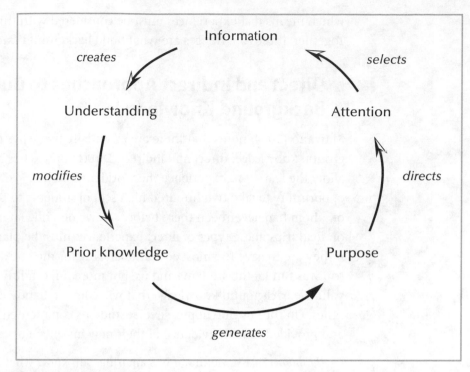

Figure 5.1 *The learning cycle*

range of other options. That is not to say that we think classrooms should be places devoid of intentional instruction; we know that teachers should provide purposeful lessons filled with guided instruction (Fisher and Frey 2008). And like Kirschner, Sweller, and Clark (2006), we are concerned when we hear that there is no intentional instruction from a teacher and that students must rely on their own discovery methods to learn.

The instruction that occurs during the information phase in Figure 5.1 (and which is based on attention, purpose, and prior knowledge) creates understanding, which in turn modifies prior knowledge. This cycle results in understanding, which is the goal of teaching. And we know that this cycle is complete—effective—when information assimilation and accommodation have occurred.

This learning cycle highlights what needs to occur for learning to happen and for it to continue to evolve. New experiences bump up against what is known to shape understanding. The processes of assimilation and accommodation need to act upon the information a learner already has, which means that experiences must be considered with this goal in mind. Together, these experiences are what build background knowledge.

■ Direct and Indirect Approaches to Building Background Knowledge

Marzano (2004) notes that there are essentially two ways to build background knowledge: direct and indirect. Direct approaches are those that allow the learner to experience the world around her. We recently had the opportunity to take two hundred high school students to Disneyland, half of whom had never been there before. As we describe later in the section on field trips, these types of direct experiences must be planned in advance if they are to have the most educational bang for the buck. And yes, the trip was fun for the students and us, but more importantly they gained valuable background knowledge that will come in handy during their lifetimes. On the bus ride home, several students commented about the trip and provided us with evidence of their new insights. For example:

Ibrahim: Splash Mountain was amazing, you know what I mean? It's not like the physics picture. The picture doesn't do justice to the force you gotta feel on the way down.

Shelene: I think it was a city. It had everything for a city: streets, stores, parks, people, everything. But a happy city with no poor people. Mostly there was happy people, except some parents who yelled at kids to have fun.

Arlisa: I wanna get a job in that parade. There were all those lights on the people walking in the parade. How did they do that? And the people were waving at them, all happy and stuff.

In addition to field trips, travel programs, mentoring, internships, college visits, after-school clubs, and sports are all effective ways for building students' funds of knowledge. Of course, students have direct experiences all of the time, but our focus as teachers is to make sure that they learn from these experiences. When we provide these types of direct experiences, we have to ensure that there is an academic focus such that background knowledge is built. Colleges and universities are recognizing the value of direct experience learning for their students, many of whom arrive with a firm academic foundation but a dearth of outside experiences. Dickinson University in New Jersey has created a direct experience program for first-year students and has studied the nonacademic effects of such an approach. Staub and Finley (2007) reported that students in programs emphasizing direct experiences had lower alcohol consumption rates, and this effect was even stronger when the direct experience program focused on civic engagement and service learning. As well, these same students were found to have fewer mental health issues.

Unfortunately, as Marzano (2004) notes, direct experiences are often limited because of the costs involved. While we acknowledge this reality, we urge teachers to find ways to ensure that students do have academically focused direct experiences in building background knowledge. This may be as simple as meeting a group of students at the park and people watching or calling a local theatre for discount, off-night tickets to a play. We take every opportunity we can to engage students in academically focused direct experiences to build background knowledge.

Indirect experiences, on the other hand, involve building background in surrogate ways. Indirect experiences include teacher modeling, wide reading, accruing and organizing information and concepts on graphic organizers, and bringing in guest speakers. We suggest using a range of direct and indirect ways to build students' background knowledge.

■ Systems for Building Background Knowledge

Alvermann writes, "Adolescents respond to the literacy demands of their subject area classes when they have appropriate background knowledge and strategies for reading a variety of texts" (2001, 8). As teachers, we have to build students' background knowledge because reading comprehension strategies alone will not result in deeper understanding of texts.

Modeling Through Think-Alouds

Teacher modeling is a powerful way for engaging students in learning. When we model, students have an example of the thinking and vocabulary required of task. Modeling is an effective way for teaching reading comprehension, writing, and problem solving (Haston 2007; Methe and Hintze 2003; VandeWagne 2006). When they model, teachers can demonstrate how they utilize text features and text structures to comprehend, as well as the ways they marshal problem-solving approaches to deal with unfamiliar vocabulary (Fisher, Frey, and Lapp 2008).

This appears to be particularly critical when a student is learning a second language, and the need for such direct instruction rises in contrast to the amount of background knowledge she possesses. Pulido (2007) examined the interaction between background knowledge, familiarity with lexical (text) features, and comprehension of ninety-nine English language learners. Not surprisingly, those who read about familiar topics were able to recall information two days later at higher rates than those who read about an unfamiliar topic. In addition, those who had less knowledge about the vocabulary and lexical features also had poor recall.

But modeling also provides teachers with an opportunity to build students' background knowledge. Ding (2008) described a cognitive apprenticeship approach to teaching college students technical writing. He noted that an instructional pattern of modeling, scaffolding, and coaching about the rules, components, and expectations of this writing genre resulted in higher-quality writing. He also acknowledged the demand modeling places on the teacher, noting that it

> requires instructors to take the position of mentors and performing experts and to model step by step their own approaches to disciplinary writing. They can offer inventive heuristics, conceptual mapping, and task overviews for writing activities so that students can focus on ways to accomplish smaller sub-tasks rather than feeling overwhelmed by the larger task. (44)

Modeling processes for learning is especially effective for building background knowledge. Alfassi (2004) conducted two studies with a total of more than three hundred ninth and tenth graders combining reciprocal teaching and direct explanation approaches. Teachers modeled aspects of reciprocal teaching, a collaborative procedure where four students read and discuss a text framed by four processes: questioning, clarifying, summarizing, and predicting (Palincsar and Brown 1984). The teachers in the study also modeled their own text comprehension with direct explanation that included thinking aloud (Duffy et al. 1987). Alfassi (2004) found that the combination of reciprocal teaching with direct explanation resulted in gains on measures of reading achievement, and that the greatest gains were among those students who possessed or activated little background knowledge.

Every year, Stephanie Raphael's tenth-grade biology students are nervous and a bit leery about the frog dissection lab. Some students have ethical objections, while others are just squeamish. For the last few years, she has been introducing the dissection process using simulation software that allows her to demonstrate the basic principles of dissection. This allows her to build background knowledge about how to properly conduct the lab so that students can focus on what they are observing when it comes time for them to dissect their own frogs. She also uses the software as an alternative assignment for students who do not want to complete the lab with real frogs.

One day Stephanie projected a ventral image of a preserved frog and observed, "The frog is on the dissection pan, and I know the first thing I need to do is pin it so that it is secure. I know the bottom of the pan has a waxy layer, so the pins will stay in." Using her cursor, she clicked on the box of dissection pins and carried a pin to each of the frog's limbs.

"I have to open the frog, but I remember that there are really two layers. The first is a skin layer, and I expect that it will be very thin. I don't need to put my pressure on the scalpel." She clicked on a scalpel on the screen and drew a cut from the sternum to the abdomen and then horizontally two more times across the upper and lower trunk. As she pinned back the skin layer, she directed the students. "Talk to your partner and describe the next layer. When you're dissecting, you always want to be thinking about what will come next." Most of them correctly predicted that the muscle layer would be next, so Stephanie continued.

"Great! You're thinking ahead to your next move. I expect that the muscle layer will be thicker and more fibrous, because that is the consistency of muscle tissue. Hmmm, that scalpel isn't going to do the trick. I need to match the tool to the task. That's why I'll choose dissection scissors this time."

Stephanie continued for the next ten minutes, moving through four layers of internal organs and thinking aloud about their structure, placement, and function. During her think-aloud, Stephanie made her problem-solving skills transparent to her students and modeled the use of academic language. In addition, she exhibited the professional and respectful demeanor she expected of them when they were working with their frogs. As she concluded with a virtual cleanup, she reminded them that as biologists their respect for all forms of life was essential and invited students to sign up for either the virtual or lab-based dissection. She told us later, "The most important thing for them to learn is how life systems work. With the advancements in technology, virtual dissection labs are becoming a viable option for students who might otherwise have made sure they were absent on lab day. Also, it's a great tool for me to model my thinking as a biologist. I couldn't have done this to the same effect ten years ago."

Importantly, the content of teacher modeling morphs into background knowledge for students as they proceed with the experience themselves.

Students can draw on their experiences with the teacher sharing her thinking and use that in new situations.

Wide Reading

While modeling provides students with examples of the types of background knowledge necessary and conditions for activating that knowledge, wide reading directly builds that knowledge. In fact, wide reading is one of the cheapest and easiest ways for people, especially struggling readers, to rapidly build their understanding (Fisher and Ivey 2006). In the absence of direct experiences, it's the most effective way for building background knowledge (Johnson 1982; Marzano 2004). Remember Doug's experience in the neuroanatomy class? Wide reading provided him with background knowledge to be successful in class.

There are a number of reasons for this. First, as explained by Cullinan (1989), literature is both a window into the world and a mirror of it. Through literature, readers learn about people they might never meet and visit places they may never travel to. These windows build amazing knowledge bases that readers can draw upon later. Who can forget their first trip to Hogwarts School of Witchcraft (Rowling 1997)? And how could we not have Charlotte of the famous web (White 1952) in our lives? In addition to viewing the world through literature, readers also see themselves in literature. Like looking in a mirror, reading literature provides the reader an opportunity to reflect. In terms of background knowledge, this mirror function serves to validate and affirm the experiences readers have had with the world. And it's painfully obvious when our students cannot find books that reflect their world. We can't even count the number of times we've been asked, "Do you know a good book about X?" when the topic has been completely predictable based on what we've known about the student. Amanda, a goth dresser who identifies as straight-edge (not a drug user), regularly asks for books about punk bands, whereas Sean, a skilled soccer player, asks for books about his sport and famous players. That's not to say that Amanda and Sean read only these books, but their choices do reflect their need to the see themselves in literature.

Second, reading volume is directly related to reading skill. The seminal research of Stanovich (1986) introduced the concept of the Matthew effect, drawn from the biblical quote about the rich getting richer while the poor get poorer. In the mid-'80s Stanovich challenged the field to consider an alternative perspective on why students who demonstrate early reading failure continue to fall behind, suggesting that "some of individual differences in cognitive processes that are associated with reading problems in the adult . . . may be remnants of reading histories of the subjects" (395).

The Mathew effect principle was borne out in a longitudinal study of twenty-seven students from their entry in first grade through the end of their junior year in high school. Even after controlling for effects like cognitive ability, Cunningham and Stanovich (1997) found that the amount of exposure to print over the previous decade of schooling was a strong predictor of reading ability and played a role in the likelihood that a student would develop a habit of reading. This has a huge impact on the background knowledge students bring into your classroom. It should be noted that these findings also predicted the amount of declarative knowledge a student possessed.

To middle and high school educators, it might appear impossible to reverse the reading histories of adolescents. However, the answer lies in creating opportunities to read through the practice of wide reading. There are a number of ways to implement wide reading, but they cluster into two major categories: sustained silent reading and independent reading. Figure 5.2 provides a comparison between these two instructional routines.

Sustained Silent Reading

Commonly known by its initials, SSR is dedicated time during the school day when students engage in reading of their own choice (Fisher 2004). This may be implemented schoolwide during a single time of the day, as when everyone in the school simultaneously engages in reading. Other schools may dedicate time in a particular course, most commonly the English class. Our experience is that the former is more effective than the latter. The daily act of everyone in the school—the principal, the front office staff, the counselors—setting aside work to make reading a priority sends a powerful message to students and the larger community.

Of course, SSR doesn't just happen, and it requires the same careful planning that any other schoolwide initiative deserves. The guidelines created by Pilgreen (2000) through her meta-analysis of thirty-two SSR studies have proven to be the touchstone for schools all over the country.

- *Access*: SSR programs require a large volume of reading materials. Not just books but magazines, newspapers, comics, pamphlets—anything that might be of interest. Some high schools we have worked with have a standing order with the department of motor vehicles for free copies of the driver's education manual. You can imagine how quickly these disappear.

	Sustained Silent Reading	**Independent Reading**
Goal	Reading for pleasure	Reading for knowledge acquisition
Text Choice	Students select from an unlimited range of possible reading materials	Students choose from a constrained list identified by the teacher
Text Difficulty	Student alone determines whether text meets her needs	Texts may be differentiated to meet range of reading levels in the classroom
Text Topic	Wide range of topics within school and district guidelines	Topic selected by teacher as part of curricular emphasis
Accountability	No book reports or assigned reading logs	Assignments may include reading logs, written summaries, discussion groups
Teacher Role	Reading while students read and holding brief conferences with individual students	Conferring with students on reading topic and administering informal assessments

Figure 5.2 *Comparing sustained silent reading and independent reading*

- *Appeal*: Appeal goes hand in hand with access. The reading materials need to be of interest to readers. Of course, they can bring their own reading materials, but this takes time. We've collected lots of interesting materials from community book drives. Just be sure you check them all carefully. We once got a medical textbook of human sexuality that no doubt would have been of great interest to our students!

- *Conducive Environment*: Pilgreen recommends a "personal and homey" environment that doesn't detract from the reading experience (10). Comfortable furnishings, a "Do Not Disturb" sign on the door, and a quiet atmosphere make reading for pleasure a possibility.

- *Encouragement*: Here's where the involvement of teaching and nonteaching staff really pays off. Students at Hoover High School enrolled in the video technology class made monthly commercials that were broadcast on closed-circuit television to motivate and inform everyone about an aspect of the SSR program.

- *Staff Training*: In our opinion, training is the linchpin of a successful SSR program. Teachers and administrators need to hash through the issues related to SSR: What is the best time of day to hold SSR? Are there materials that can't be read? What do you do with a student who refuses to participate? The most successful schools we've worked with keep SSR as a standing topic for every faculty meeting. Even though it occupies only five to ten minutes of the meeting, it allows for timely problem solving.

- *Nonaccountability*: This is often viewed as the most controversial element. After all, who will read if he doesn't have to do anything with the reading? The answer, as it turns out, is virtually everyone. When was the last time you had to write a book report for your Thursday night book club? Does your spouse require you to submit a summary of the interesting newspaper article you just read aloud over the breakfast table? Of course not. There's lots of time in the school day for assignments. Just not during SSR.

- *Follow-Up Activities*: This differs from typical assignments such as reading logs with page numbers and book summaries. Pilgreen encourages the kind of natural activities that follow a good read. Giving a book talk, making a recommendation—these sharing activities encourage the community of readers you're building.

- *Distributed Time to Read*: We all learned in our teacher education programs that distributed practice beats mass practice every time, and reading is no different. Just as cramming the night before a test is less effective than shorter, but more frequent, study sessions, SSR should be held daily, preferably at the same time. The goal is to establish a habit of reading, and this simply can't happen if SSR is once a week. Better to devote fifteen to twenty minutes daily than sixty minutes every Friday.

Independent Reading

It's easy to confuse independent reading with SSR, because both of them feature student choice. However, in independent reading, the choice is limited to materials selected by the teacher that match the curricular and learner goals of the unit. Independent reading is commonly offered as a component of a reading or writing workshop model and thus is designed to augment the modeling that begins each lesson and the guided instruction and conferring that occurs in small groups while the rest of the class is reading (e.g., Atwell 1998).

What students read really depends on the goals of the class. For students in English language arts, the need often focuses on genres and understanding the essential features of various genres. Lisa Jesperson requires that

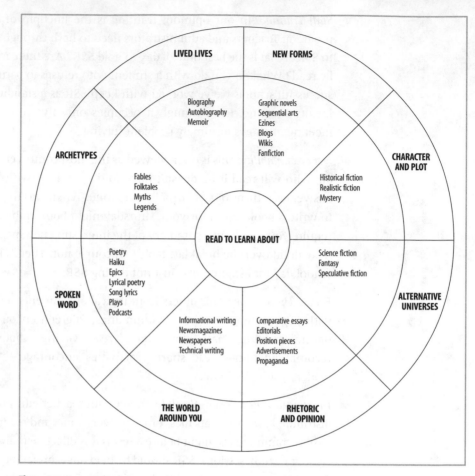

Figure 5.3 *Genre wheel*

The genre wheel contains the following sections radiating from a central hub labeled **READ TO LEARN ABOUT**:

- **LIVED LIVES**: Biography, Autobiography, Memoir
- **NEW FORMS**: Graphic novels, Sequential arts, Ezines, Blogs, Wikis, Fanfiction
- **ARCHETYPES**: Fables, Folktales, Myths, Legends
- **CHARACTER AND PLOT**: Historical fiction, Realistic fiction, Mystery
- **SPOKEN WORD**: Poetry, Haiku, Epics, Lyrical poetry, Song lyrics, Plays, Podcasts
- **ALTERNATIVE UNIVERSES**: Science fiction, Fantasy, Speculative fiction
- **THE WORLD AROUND YOU**: Informational writing, Newsmagazines, Newspapers, Technical writing
- **RHETORIC AND OPINION**: Comparative essays, Editorials, Position pieces, Advertisements, Propaganda

students read from at least 50 percent of the book types on a genre wheel (see Figure 5.3) each quarter. Students shade in the sections of the wheel as they complete different books and write the title of each book off to the side of the wheel. During her conferences with students, Lisa asks about favorite genres and the characteristics of each genre read during the term.

Remember Amanda, the avid reader of punk history? During her conversation with Lisa, she talked about the different books she had read and how they had contributed to her understanding. Let's listen in on their conversation.

Amanda: I was all about the war this quarter because of my dad. I've been reading in different genres because they tell you different parts of the experience. Like I read a couple graphic novels like *Pride of*

Baghdad [Vaughan and Henrichon 2008] and *The 9/11 Commission Report* [Jacobson and Colon 2006]. So far, I also read realistic fiction, *Sunrise over Fallujah* [Myers 2008] and a biography, well, journals and letters anyway, called *Boredom by Day, Death by Night: An Iraq War Journal* [Conner 2007]. And I found a collection of poems about war in the library called *American War Poetry: An Anthology* [Goldensohn 2006].

Lisa: I have lots of questions for you because you have such an interesting collection. Which was the best? What did you learn from these? How does the genre influence your understanding of the war? Choose any one of those to talk about.

Amanda: I think that the graphic novels helped me really get a picture of what is going on where my dad is. I was mad about him going, but the *9/11 [Commission] Report* made me think a little about responsibility. The poems didn't do much for me, but I'm glad I read them. I even gave one to my mom. The diary and letters made me very sad and probably hit me the most. That book made me make sure that I wrote to my dad every day.

Lisa: Do you want to talk further about how it made you feel? Or do you want to talk about something else?

Amanda: Is it OK if we don't talk about it right now, but we can later?

Lisa: Yes, of course.

Amanda: Can you help me find another genre?

The English teacher was pleased with Amanda's progress with the genres she had read. During this semester, Amanda had read several selections from the new forms category, as well as the information genre. She had chosen books from the character and plot genre and had even tried spoken word. She and Lisa decided that the next reading should come from the rhetoric genre, so that Amanda could apply her growing background knowledge to some editorials and position pieces. Amanda's reading, focused by genre for her English class, conveys the power of wide reading in building background knowledge. The books she read influenced her thinking about major world events. True, she had a stake in those events, and the reading compelled her to action. Her interest in local and national elections was awakened, and she became involved in a voter registration drive.

Like Lisa, Sean Andrews uses reading to build his students' background knowledge. As a sixth-grade social studies teacher, Sean knows that most

Lassieur, A. 2005. *The Ancient Romans*. London: Franklin Watts.

Mellor, R., and M. McGee. 2004. *The Ancient Roman World*. New York: Oxford University Press.

Nardo, D. 2001. *Lost Civilizations: The Ancient Romans*. Chicago: Lucent Books.

Roberts, T. R. 2000. *Ancient Rome: History of a Civilization That Ruled the World*. New York: Metrobooks.

Solway, A., and P. Connolly. 2001. *Ancient Rome*. New York: Oxford University Press.

Figure 5.4 *Sample books on ancient Roman civilization*

of his students are unfamiliar with the content of the class. The majority of sixth graders do not arrive with deep reservoirs of knowledge about ancient Egypt, Greek and Roman civilization, or the contributions of African and Asian ancient cultures. To quickly build their background knowledge, Sean collects books on specific topics identified in the content standards and invites students to read for ten minutes each day during class time. The collected books span a difficulty range of about six years (between second- and eighth-grade difficulty) and include a number of genres. On a daily basis, students select books from the collection to read independently. For example, some of the books related to ancient Roman civilization are listed in Figure 5.4.

The logistics of this approach to building background knowledge can be tricky. We know that books are expensive. Sean addresses this issue by using library books and combing used bookstores and the swap meet. The librarian allows books from the general collection to be temporarily stored in classrooms during specific units of study. For example, when they're studying ancient Egypt, Sean adds *The Atlas of Ancient Egypt* (Pemberton 2005) to his classroom collection. When the unit of study has been completed, he returns library books for regular circulation.

Another barrier is storage. Sean addresses this by storing the book collections in file boxes in the department office. He has only the books for the current unit in his classroom. This also prevents the books from being damaged mistakenly as students rifle through book stacks looking for something to read. And finally, independent reading can present a management challenge. Sean addresses this during the first week of school, in which students practice the behaviors expected of them as readers and thinkers. Sean knows that students have to be explicitly taught the instructional routines expected in a classroom and that these routines should be regularly reviewed and reinforced if they are to remain in practice (Frey 2007).

Graphic Organizers

How often have you asked someone to "picture this" when explaining an event? Or perhaps you've checked a friend's understanding by asking him, "Do you see what I mean?" While these may be figures of speech, they do illustrate the role of visual and spatial information in learning. Even that last sentence relied on the words *figure* and *illustrate*!

Most of us depend on visual representations of information to interpret our world. Iconographic signs tell us which restroom to use and create boundaries for safely crossing a street. Health care workers use visual dictionaries to confirm medical diagnoses. (If you want to keep yourself awake at night worrying about skin conditions, visit www.visualdxhealth.com/). We used the Visual Thesaurus as we wrote this book (available at www.visualthesaurus.com/) to quickly identify synonyms for overused words.

Knowledge doesn't reside in a specific part of the brain; it is distributed throughout. While language-based information is primarily in the left hemisphere, nonverbal representations lie in the right. Typical classroom instruction relies heavily on language-based knowledge, with relatively little attention paid to other forms. However, studies in several disciplines point to the importance of visual and spatial knowledge in learning. For instance, a study of people with both high and low levels of knowledge about meteorology found that their ability to interpret weather maps was significantly influenced by their visual-spatial ability to understand maps (Allen, Cowan, and Power 2006). Schonborn and Anderson (2006) make a case that visual knowledge is essential to the learning of biochemists.

The evidence on the effectiveness of graphic displays of information for building understanding dates back to the 1960s and has been linked to reading comprehension (Hegarty, Carpenter, and Just 1991) and cognition (Winn 1991). More recently, Vekiri (2002) conducted a thorough review of the research on visual displays, described as diagrams, maps, tables, and charts. She noted that the research on graphic displays, which is extracted from the fields of neuroscience and cognitive science, suggests that attention must be given to design principles and learner characteristics. She makes the following design recommendations (275–76):

- *Displays need to address the goals of the task.* For example, when the goal is to help students understand cause-effect relations or how systems behave, diagrams need to show not only the components of the systems but also how they interact and interrelate.

- *Displays should be provided along with explanations and guidance.* Graphics contribute to learning when students [are] guided by questions for practice or prompts that [encourage] interaction with the displays. . . . Such techniques may cue attention to relevant details.

- *Displays need to be spatially and timely coordinated with text.* Concurrent use of verbal and visual material can help learners develop richer and more coherent mental models because they can form connections between what is presented in graphics and in text.

Vekiri also produces evidence that the characteristics of the learner influence how effectively graphic organizers can be used, especially when it comes to background knowledge. There is some conflicting information, with some researchers reporting that those with lower levels of background knowledge benefited more than those with high levels (Mayer and Gallini 1990), while other studies showed the opposite effect (Hegarty, Carpenter, and Just 1991) because of the ability of higher-performing students to extract information more efficiently. It would seem, however, that the graphic organizer should not contain too much textual information, as this creates a burden on the learner, whether she has a low or high level of background knowledge (Tukey 1990).

Sixth-grade social studies teacher Sean Andrews introduced his students to the ancient Greek philosopher Aristotle and planned to further build their background knowledge about his contributions to history. He wanted to make sure they learned that Aristotle drew from several knowledge bases to form new ideologies. In particular, he identified this as core knowledge for the unit and wanted them to use what they knew about the arts and sciences to build this new schema.

He planned to use a graphic organizer to illustrate the modes of persuasive argument first outlined by Aristotle: *logos*, *ethos*, and *pathos*. Sean began by telling his students about a neighbor of his who let her dog run loose. He listed the problems it caused, especially that the dog frightened his young children and that he didn't like cleaning up his yard after the animal had been there. Sean also explained that the elderly man who lived across the street was frail and could be easily knocked over by the dog. He made a list of the possible arguments that he could use in his conversation with the dog owner.

"I could tell her that there is a law that prohibits dog owners from having their pets off a leash or in an unsecured location," he mused. "Then I could tell her about the fines she could get."

"No way she'd like hearing that, Mr. A.," said Joshua. "She'd probably get in your face if you started with that."

"Good point. Maybe I should start by explaining that I am the Neighborhood Watch captain for our block and that I have some concerns about her dog," the teacher replied.

"That would get her attention, for sure. She might listen better," Kaylin said. "Then you can tell her about the old man across the street, and how your little kids get afraid," she added.

"This is shaping up to be a great plan for persuading her. I could end the conversation with the information about how it's against the law, if I need it," Sean said. He finished making his notes on the whiteboard.

With that, he shifted gears and distributed a graphic organizer to use in the next part of the lesson (see Figure 5.5). He explained that Aristotle was a man who thought a lot about the best ways to persuade people and that he had developed the concepts of *logos*, *pathos*, and *ethos*. Using the pictures for immediate recognition, he explained each. The students then categorized his list of arguments using the space on the graphic organizer. By taking the

Appeal	Definition	Example
Logos	A deliberate appeal to the reader's sense of logic and need for factual proof or reasonable sense	*It is against the law to let a dog run free and you could be fined.*
Ethos	A conscientious appeal to the reader's appreciation of credentials or professional experience	*I am the Neighborhood Watch captain and it is my job to keep the block safe.*
Pathos	A deliberate appeal to the reader's emotions, including pity, sympathy, fear, guilt, compassion, or love	*There is an elderly man who could get knocked over, and my little kids are afraid of the dog.*

Figure 5.5 *Rhetorical appeals graphic organizer*

time to build some background knowledge, the teacher readied them for the more demanding textbook passage about Aristotle and his philosophical contributions to persuasive thought.

Guest Speakers

Although schooling has always been a community function, most of us overlook the human resources available to us in our town or city. Guest speakers provide us with the opportunity to bring history, science, and the humanities into our classrooms in the form of people who have lived these experiences. A guest speaker can also, by his or her presence, address the classic question "When will I ever need to know this?"

Anatomy and physiology teacher Gail Wortman refers to guest speakers as "an invitation to learn" for exactly this reason (1992, 19). Whether listening to a dermatologist discuss the dangers of tanning beds during their unit on the skin or watching an audiologist demonstrate how an inner ear is viewed using an otoscope, her students are able to see firsthand how the concepts they are learning in the classroom are applied in practice.

Criminal justice instructors Payne, Sumter, and Sun (2003) state that the guest speakers they invite into their classrooms are able to achieve three goals:

- bring the field into the classroom;

- open students minds' to varying viewpoints; and

- alter students' attitudes and perceptions in favorable ways. (336)

They also advise that careful preparation before, during, and after the visit is essential if students are to derive the full benefit. First, you should carefully select the speaker, preferably one you have personally seen before. Since the person will be carrying the class for a period of time, she needs to be an effective communicator. You must also prepare the speaker so that she will have a good sense of what the class knows and does not know about the topic. The class should be prepared for the guest speaker as well. There's nothing worse than having a speaker walk in cold to a class where the students know nothing about her. When we use guest speakers, we discuss the person's background in advance and ask our students to prepare questions. We find that this activates their background knowledge and leaves them with something to say when the speaker asks, "Any questions?" We use some of this time to discuss etiquette and ways to demonstrate appreciation. After the speaker leaves, we follow up with a letter to her and send a copy to the speaker's supervisor or employer.

Eileen O'Hearn invites members of the community into her tenth-grade geometry classroom several times a year to discuss how they use geometric principles in their daily work. These include an architect, a highway engineer, and an owner of a tree-cutting service, who demonstrates how he finds the height of a tree using triangulation. One of her favorite speakers is her brother, Sean, who is a master tile setter. During an early unit on tessellation patterns, Eileen asks Sean to stop by to explain how he sets tile in bathrooms and kitchens using principles of geometry. He shows the students photographs of the work done by his company and shares his notes and plans from previous jobs. With Ms. O'Hearn's help, the students use graph paper and small tiles in a multitude of shapes and colors to create unique tessellations of their own. As part of their follow-up, her students investigate the use of tiling in other cultures and gather examples of tessellations from Islamic architecture, in Escher prints, and in optical illusions.

Field Trips At the beginning of this chapter we mentioned a field trip to Disneyland, a place many of our students had never been before, despite its location less than two hours north of our school. The curriculum is centered on health sciences, which has become a critical-need field in the last decade. The Disneyland trip came at the end of the school year, but would it surprise you to learn that we held a field trip for the entire school during the first week of the academic year? The logistics were daunting (all those permission forms!), but it was essential for rapidly building the background knowledge of the student body.

We knew that most of the students would be arriving at our school with little background knowledge about the science of the human body, but we were fortunate that Bodies: The Exhibition was being held in our city. This exhibit of human cadavers that have been preserved using a polymer process is arranged to highlight various body systems, including the skeletal, circulatory, and nervous systems. We spent the first few days of school preparing our students for the field trip, including behavioral expectations and academic goals. The biology teachers went to the exhibition in advance and prepared an interactive study guide for students to complete as they traveled in small groups with adults through the exhibit. Their scientific knowledge of the human body grew a great deal that day and allowed their teachers to reap the benefits for the rest of the year.

Obviously, field trips should not be treated as a novel experience, and the follow-up is just as important as the planning that goes into the logistics.

However, this field trip allowed teachers in content areas other than science to build and activate students' background knowledge. For example, the English teachers taught persuasive writing and research skills as they examined the controversy surrounding the provenance of the cadavers, and history teachers were able to frame the controversy within the context of the rapid changes occurring in China regarding the acquisition of cadavers. We found that the students responded positively to the exhibition, even as they raised questions about ethical and medical issues.

Teachers must examine the learning potential of a possible field trip to determine if it is a good use of classroom time. The field trip should emphasize interaction with concepts, not just passive viewing. Farmer, Knapp, and Benton (2006) measured the retention of children who had attended a field trip to the George Washington Carver Memorial a year earlier. They discovered that the concepts most likely to be recalled were those that required the students to take action, such as crushing soybeans to make soymilk and engaging with interactive museum displays.

While districts and schools have their own procedures for arranging field trips, it is useful to keep several principles in mind to get the most from these events. Kisiel (2006) makes the following recommendations:

- *Make connections.* The first consideration is how the trip will relate to curriculum, so that you can plan before and after experiences.

- *Research ahead of time.* The logistics of even a small field trip can be daunting, so contact the venue in advance and talk to the education director. This prevents misunderstandings and doesn't put the venue in the difficult position of having a large group show up unexpectedly.

- *Prepare students.* "Hands-on doesn't mean brains off," says one of our favorite science teachers, so make sure that students understand that this is a day of school and that they will be accountable for their learning. We find that task sheets are a tangible reminder of the focus on learning.

- *Prepare chaperones.* Let them know how they can help with the learning, not just crowd management. Give them questions to ask on the bus or a review sheet of what will occur and how it relates to curricular learning.

- *Follow up.* Keep the experience alive in the classroom by writing about it, discussing it, and sharing it with other classes. You took the time to build this background knowledge, but it will be for naught if there is little follow-up.

Extended Out-of-School Learning

While the types of experiences that extend across the school year are less common because of their expense, they cannot be overlooked for their value in building background knowledge. We have been directly involved in two such projects, each with very different goals. The first was School in the Park, a collaborative project between Rosa Parks Elementary School and the museums of Balboa Park in San Diego (Pumpian, Fisher, and Wachowiak 2006). Originally conceived for practical purposes (an overcrowded school campus), School in the Park blossomed into a three-year curriculum for third through fifth graders. They attended a museum classroom for an entire week each month, where museum educators and classroom teachers delivered math, English, science, social studies, and art instruction. The paintings of the art museum, for instance, provided an opportunity to teach third graders about story structure. Students created their own narrative paintings about a fictitious fourteenth-century character named Giovanni and wrote his story in words (Frey 2006). The three years of museum-based education afforded these students with valuable background knowledge about the social, biological, and physical worlds around them, as they learned how the content of their classes was developed.

For older students, internships have proven to be valuable to making connections between school and career. Long used as a bridge between classroom learning and professions like law, medicine, and education, internships are becoming more common at the high school level, especially as a way to increase student engagement. Students who attend our school participate in assigned weekly hospital internships to learn all aspects of health care. Before they can go, they must complete a list of requirements, including training in cardiopulmonary resuscitation (CPR), maintaining patient confidentiality, patient transport and body mechanics, and hand-washing procedures. Liaisons from the hospitals work in conjunction with school staff to teach and certify each student on these requirements.

Students at the hospital wear scrubs and identification and accompany a preceptor in small groups of three to six. During one year they completed patient care rotations in ophthalmology, pain management, heart catheterization, pediatrics, labor and delivery, rehabilitation services, and nursing. They also worked in non–patient care areas, such as sterilizing equipment, preparing patient meals, and working in the pathology lab.

While the experiences students had there are too numerous to recount here, we will describe an event that occurred in late fall that year. The students had been attending internships for about six weeks, after completing their prerequisite certifications. One of the students had been working in the heart catheterization lab when a patient crashed during the procedure. The woman stopped breathing and went into cardiac arrest. Despite the efforts of the medical team, the woman died. This was the first time one of our students had been in the room when someone had died, and we weren't quite sure how any of them would react. We weren't sure how we would react, either.

The student returned to school at the end of the day, and we were there to debrief with her. She had already had an opportunity to talk at the hospital with a school administrator who accompanies students on their internships. Our student gently explained what had occurred, and while she was visibly moved by the situation, we were amazed at her professional demeanor and her ability to keep her composure. She told us, "Everything you taught us happened. I knew exactly what was going on, so even though it was hard, I understood. They called code blue, the crash cart came, and everyone worked together to do what they could for this woman." She paused for a moment and then said, "I couldn't understand why you were making us learn all this stuff, why we couldn't just start going to the hospital the first week. But now I get it. I knew what I was seeing, and I wasn't afraid because I understood."

A few months later, we revisited this moment with her. "I'm going to be a cardiologist," she said. "That day told me that this is what I am supposed to do with my life."

■ Conclusion

There is so much we can do as teachers to accelerate our students' acquisition of knowledge. Once we move away from the idea that building background knowledge is a matter of pouring information into students' brains, we can connect to a kind of teaching that is active, is constructive, and brings the world in to enrich our students. The action word *building* is key to understanding that knowledge is the product of an active process resulting from experiences that continually bump up against what is known. Whether you call this assimilation and accommodation, as Piaget did, or whether you prefer thinking of it as meaningful learning, the result is information that can be applied by the student to new situations (transfer).

Therefore, we can't think of building background as just telling them what they need to know; they need to experience it in countless ways.

Much of this happens in the classroom as they witness how an expert (the teacher) solves learning problems using his own background knowledge. They also bump into their own learning through wide reading. The information one encounters in a book that will end up being used later cannot be quantified, but we recognize it each time it happens. A student tells us about a book, or surprises us with a piece of information we didn't know, and we immediately think, "She's well read."

Finally, students can learn through direct experiences that challenge their notions about the relevancy of classroom learning. Guest speakers can bring the wider world to them as they share their experiences and discuss how the background knowledge gained in the classroom plays out in their work lives. Carefully crafted field trips can rapidly expand the student knowledge base and provide shared experiences that can be drawn on months later. And extended out-of-school learning through internships can connect school and career together for adolescents who are constantly challenging the relevancy of classroom learning.

None of these is easily accomplished. The word *building* is associated with hard work and heavy lifting. Likewise, the hard work of building background knowledge requires that teachers, the architects of their students' learning, create experiences that cause students to bump into, and reconsider, what they know.

Critical Literacy

Helping Students Get Beyond the Sift-and-Surf
Mode to Deep Synthesis of Texts

IN HER CAPACITY AS AN ADVISOR to a high school newspaper, Nancy meets with student journalists and editors to discuss ideas for stories, perform fact checking, and proofread for stylistic consistency. During a planning meeting for the second issue of the year, a ninth-grade reporter, Jenna, arrived with an article she had already written. Now here are some things you need to know about Jenna: She is a very good student, and a B is a rare occurrence for her. She is conscientious about her work and thoughtful in giving a hand to classmates who could use a boost. She's the kind of student most teachers wish for every year and the sort of daughter that other parents point to when they are lovingly trying to coerce their own children about something!

Now put yourself in Nancy's shoes. Imagine that Jenna has just handed you an article she is very proud of and that she clearly feels invested in. And imagine what's going through your mind as you read her story about Mahatma Mohandas Gandhi. The story opens with a grabber that gains the reader's attention: check. It integrates powerful quotes into the story: check. Sources are cited: check. But here's the problem: the story is based on scurrilous information that alleges Gandhi harbored a secret hatred of other races and that he supported the caste system as a way of keeping India pure. What's your next move?

In this case, Nancy set aside the article so she could discuss it with Jenna and the editor of the school newspaper in a private meeting. Later in the day the three met and Nancy told Jenna that she was concerned about the piece because it contained information that she hadn't been able to verify. She asked Jenna where she'd gotten her information, because that might help with fact checking. Jenna logged onto a computer and began pulling up websites that contained the information she had used in her article. "I didn't know this stuff, either," she said as she clicked through the links. "But here it is. This is the kind of stuff they don't teach you in history books."

"It's not in history books because it's not sound history," Nancy stammered, but as she answered, she had the sensation of sliding on black ice. She realized anew that Internet use in education is a vast, slippery terrain. In the rush and demands of teaching, it's hard to take the time to teach students about using its resources well. Nancy counseled Jenna on the American Society for Newspaper Editors' (ASNE) standards for verifying sources and the need for outside documentation when making allegations against someone. Jenna left the meeting understanding that the article couldn't be used in the school newspaper, but Nancy felt as though she'd left Jenna in the dark.

In the days that followed, Nancy mulled next steps for teaching Jenna—and all students. How might she help them sharpen their ability to question information, bring their own background knowledge to bear while they read information, and form critical judgments? To some extent, having a nose for substandard journalism and erroneous information comes with time, age, and world experience, and we can't expect our middle and high school students to have quite the same critical sharpness. But that said, we can take them a long way there with direct teaching about reading with a critical eye. We can point out common red flags that warn us of opinions cloaked as facts and we can share with students the hallmarks of quality, fair-minded reporting—whether online, in a newspaper, in a video, or wherever.

For example, Nancy worked with Jenna more closely to investigate online sources and modeled her own thinking for Jenna as she analyzed the quality of information found on websites. She showed Jenna how to identify sources of information, such as reading the "About Us" section of a web page and considering the domain (e.g., .gov, .edu, .com). Jenna, for her part, acquired a more sophisticated set of skills for questioning what she encountered but remained vulnerable to the commonly held belief that if it's on the Internet, it must be true.

Jenna's naïveté about Internet sources illustrates the two central ideas educators face in teaching their students. The first is that now more than ever, students need to critically analyze what they read and view, always considering who created it and for what purposes. The second idea is really an extension of the first: digital access to information and disinformation has raised the stakes considerably because of its immediacy and the extent to which it reaches a vast readership. And without the first, the second leaves our students unguarded and easily subjugated.

In order for Jenna to make more sophisticated judgments about the information she read in books and on the Internet, viewed on television, and heard in conversations with others, she needed to be able to make critical assessments. Sagacity, the ability to form an opinion by evaluating more than one perspective, is essential. And Jenna's ability to be more sagacious was directly tied to both her existing background knowledge and her adeptness at building her funds of knowledge. In short, Nancy needed to strengthen Jenna's capacity to pose questions of text and not merely accept what she read at face value. For Jenna to do so, she also had to ask what was not being represented, because the absence of information carries meaning as well. This positioning, called critical literacy, challenges educators to show their students how to activate, build, and assess their own background knowledge in order to reach new understandings. At the end of this chapter, we return to Nancy's work with this student to foster a critical literacy stance.

In this chapter, we seek to move the conversation about background knowledge to a new level. As teachers of adolescents and citizens of the world, we are concerned that the emphasis on declarative knowledge (facts) has pushed conditional knowledge (knowing when and why to apply information) to the side. Further, we regard critical literacy as fundamental to conditional knowledge, because this stance drives the learner's decisions about how information will be understood. In the effort to teach students *what* to think, we have not taught them *how* to think. We need to put the reins in their hands. If we are to cultivate a culture of thoughtfulness, students must be able to evaluate and critically examine the world around them.

At the heart of critical literacy are three foundational beliefs: we must understand the various influences on our thinking, question assumptions made by authors when they write, and examine the perspectives that guide our understanding. As we will explore further, critical literacy is vital in the twenty-first century. As citizens in a democracy, we are responsible for thinking deeply about the texts we read and for interrogating our assumptions and the perspectives promoted by authors. In short, citizenship requires participation, and that participation is based on an understanding that we can question without fear.

■ What Is Critical Literacy?

Critical literacy is the practice of challenging texts through an analysis of the roles that power, culture, class, and gender play in the message. Texts are approached with an understanding that multiple perspectives exist and can be influenced by the author's and the reader's experiences. McLaughlin and DeVoogd remind us that "critical literacy helps us to move beyond . . . passive acceptance and take an active role in the reader-author relationship by questioning such issues as who wrote the text, what the author wanted us to believe, and what information the author chose to include or exclude from the text" (2004, 6). Educators in Australia and New Zealand have pioneered this construct since the early 1990s, where it has grown to be an integral part of literacy education from kindergarten through the twelfth grade. The Tasmania (Australia) Department of Education describes critical literacy extensively in its content standards and frameworks, reminding teachers of three questions readers should consider:

- In whose interest?

- For what purpose?

- Who benefits? (2006, 4)

These are questions we routinely pose as adults when we read or view information. We bring a dose of healthy skepticism everywhere we go. We also anticipate resistance to information. As social progressivism author Upton Sinclair once wrote, "It is difficult to get a man to understand something, when his salary depends upon his not understanding it" (1994, 109). Therefore, we understand that the beliefs held by a person or an organization are influenced by self-preservation. This doesn't mean that they are inherently evil, but rather that one must acknowledge that beliefs sustain and preserve. The sixth-grade teachers at one middle school developed an interdisciplinary unit to ensure that their students would know how to ask these valuable questions of themselves.

Building Habits of Mind in Sixth Grade

Teachers at a middle school determined that in order for their students to be able to build their own background knowledge, they would need to teach learners how to pose questions about interest, purpose, and benefit when evaluating information. They used the three questions described in the Tasmania standards as their essential questions for the first semester of the school year. Students regularly encountered these questions throughout their school day. In mathematics Mike Jenkins conducted an extended stock market game that lasted for several weeks so that students could gain a sense of how self-interest influences economic behavior. Each team of four students was given ten thousand dollars to invest and asked to consider the questions as part of their decision-making process. In June Bey's science class, students studied symbiosis in nature. They learned about the mutually beneficial relationships between goby fish and shrimp, digestive tract bacteria and humans, and remoras and sharks. Science students also contrasted these with parasitic relationships used by some viruses, bacteria, and insects.

In Danny Martinez's social studies class, students explored the differences between Britain and the United States in 1833 when the former abolished slavery while the latter did not. Using the same central questions about interest, purpose, and benefit, they explored the transatlantic slave trade that depended on the movement of sugar, manufactured goods, and enslaved people to sustain economic development in both countries. In English, the sixth graders in Tricia Henderson's class read *Nothing but the Truth* (Avi 1993) and *The True Confessions of Charlotte Doyle* (Avi 2004) to analyze the ways characters in the books evaluated available information to arrive at a controversial decision. For the first, literature circles used the questions to determine how Philip's school misbehavior (humming during the national anthem) escalates into a national story as his parents, school administrators, and politicians each advocate for their own positions. Students reading the second novel applied these questions as they analyzed Charlotte's decision to lead a mutiny on a ship.

The intent of the sixth-grade team was to build a habit of mind for questioning phenomena in the social, physical, and biological worlds. "Habits are formed through repetition," June remarked. "We want students to automat-

ically ask these questions of themselves when they encounter information."
By asking these questions, students discovered where the gaps existed in
their background knowledge.

"I had a couple of students tell me about John Newton, the English slave
trader who disavowed human trafficking," said Danny, the social studies
teacher. "They were doing some research about Britain's abolition movement and learned that he was the man who wrote the song 'Amazing
Grace.' Because they knew the song and were learning about the history of
the time, they made some powerful connections. Suddenly, that song took
on a whole new meaning. You could just see all the pieces of the puzzle
coming together for them."

Students become critically literate through exposure to and discussion of
readings that address social, political, and cultural issues. Critically literate
students examine the beliefs and values that underpin texts, question the
purpose and the message, take a stance on issues, and formulate action steps
when needed. Luke and Freebody (1999) describe four "families of practice"
necessary for every reader to assume:

- *Code Breaker*: understanding the text at the surface level (alphabetic,
  structural)

- *Meaning Maker*: comprehending the text at the level intended by the
  author

- *Text User*: analyzing the factors that influenced the author and the text,
  including a historical grounding of the context within which it was
  written

- *Text Critic*: understanding that the text is not neutral and that existing
  biases inform calls to action

The first three are needed in order to acquire and analyze information,
especially when that information is text bound. However, the ability to acquire and analyze is not enough. Students must also know how to convert
what they know into a way of constructing new understandings. It is this
fourth practice, the text critic, that we will explore further. This is what
Jenna lacked when she wrote her article containing questionable assertions
and information about Gandhi. We hope to ensure that students develop an
understanding of the bias that exists in all texts. An African proverb puts it
another way: "Until lions have historians, hunters will be the heroes." Using
critical literacy, readers actively seek to understand what the historians say,
consider what the voiceless lions might express, evaluate both messages to

achieve a more nuanced understanding, and then use the information to take action.

■ Background Knowledge and Critical Literacy

Critical literacy is about making sure that students know what to *do* with their background knowledge and providing them a way for building their own. You'll recall from Chapter 1 that the National Research Council (2000) described three conditions that make background knowledge useable and useful: it must be organized, conditionalized, and transferable. In the same way, critical literacy is the engine that drives a learner's background knowledge from merely a list o' facts to something that is operational (conditionalized and transferable). It is this ability to use what is known to construct heuristics (methods for solving problems) that constitutes higher-order thinking.

But thinking as problem solving requires that a problem be recognized in the first place. Researchers in fields as diverse as women's studies, public health, religion, and ethics refer to this as *problematizing*—the act of consciously seeking to locate a problem where one has not traditionally been perceived. It is the intentional peeling back of layers to examine the motives and intentions of those involved. A critical approach to learning teaches students to use their background knowledge to locate, analyze, and solve problems.

The framework for critical literacy proposed by van Sluys, Lewison, and Flint (2006) is an apt way to describe the dimensions of critical literacy as an engine for problematizing and problem solving. They describe four processes of critical literacy (215):

- disrupting a common situation or understanding
- examining multiple viewpoints
- focusing on sociopolitical issues
- taking action

Disrupting the Commonplace

The first element of critical literacy is the one that comes to mind most quickly for many educators. Disruption of the commonplace typically looks at the role of race and gender in a given situation. Racial and gender identities of self and others are arguably the deepest of all background knowledge, in that they are difficult to tease apart in order to scrutinize (e.g., Gilligan

2006; Parker and Stovall 2004). In all likelihood, you have read texts like *Through My Eyes*, by Ruby Bridges (1999), an autobiographical account of her experiences as a six-year-old child being escorted through the school doors of William Frantz Elementary School in 1960, the first African American child to attend a white school in the southern United States. Books such as this provide middle school students with a glimpse of someone's actions as she disrupts a common situation.

As well, a critical examination of gender roles can occur through compelling characters in narrative. *The Breadwinner* (Ellis 2001) introduces readers to Parvana, a girl in Taliban-controlled Afghanistan who must disguise herself as a boy in order to venture into the marketplace to earn a living for her family. With her older brother dead and her father taken away, she is the only person left in the family who is old enough to work but young enough to hide her female identity. This novel has proven to be popular among middle school readers who are beginning to notice the larger political issues that fill the international landscape. Older adolescents find *Persepolis*, Marjane Satrapi's (2004) autobiographical account of her adolescence in Iran, Austria, and France during the 1970s and 1980s, compelling. The author uses a graphic novel format to describe her difficulties growing up in a country where societal and political norms were changing rapidly and violently.

Gender identity itself can be confronted in books like *Parrotfish* (Wittinger 2007), named after the fish that can change its gender. Grady (formerly Angela) is a high school junior who is adjusting to himself at the same time the world is trying to figure out what to do with him. Stories that address aspects of gender roles and identities can cause readers to step outside of themselves as they consider how their own lives are influenced by masculine and feminine expectations. Deeply rooted beliefs and assumptions about race and gender shape the way background knowledge is formed, understood, and realized. Therefore it is essential to expose students to their own assumptions so they will better understand the role they play in learning. This noticing is key to the metacognitive awareness that students require to fuel their own continued learning (see Chapter 3 for a fuller discussion on metacognition).

Each of these texts invites students to learn more about its topic because the story is constructed to shed a light on less well-known experiences. Whether exploring more about the effects of the civil rights movement on one small girl, or researching information on the use of fear by the Taliban to silence Afghani citizens, students become aware of what they don't know and are thus motivated to seek more information. This drive to find out new information lies at the heart of background knowledge. When a learner is motivated to educate herself about a topic, it is amazing what she can accomplish. Let's take a look at the effects of motivation and background knowledge on another student when his high school English teacher sought to disrupt commonplace assumptions through the use of a great work of literature.

Disrupting the Commonplace in Tenth-Grade English

"Have you ever looked in a mirror and had trouble recognizing yourself?" asked tenth-grade English teacher Nyapal Ayati. Seeing nods of agreement, the teacher continued. "One of the short stories we'll be examining embodies that same idea. The main character becomes unrecognizable to himself. Worst of all, no one around him seems to notice."

Nyapal used that question to introduce her students to Kafka's novella *The Metamorphosis* (1915/2006). However, before they delved into Kafka's work, she read them the picture book *Beetle Boy* (David 2002). This seemingly benign tale of a second grader who wakes up to discover that he has turned into a bug drew amused responses from the fifteen-year-olds. They discussed the picture book on superficial terms, remarking on the engaging illustrations and the witty dialogue between the boy and his parents, who treat his assertion that he has turned into a bug as the product of their son's vivid imagination. In other words, they evaluated the picture book only on its entertainment merits.

The following day, the teacher introduced *The Metamorphosis*. Students were in turns horrified and intrigued at the experiences of protagonist Gregor Samsa, who awakens one morning to discover that he has been transformed into giant insect. Having lost the ability to speak, he is not able to share his agony with his family, who are merely disgusted by his appearance and lock him in his room.

After reading and discussing the more conventional aspects of the novella for the next few lessons, including symbolism, tone, and vocabulary, Nyapal used the text to explore deeper themes. In particular, she invited students to consider why the author might have written such a disturbing story. They soon concluded that they didn't have enough information about Kafka or the era to reach any conclusions. "So what do you need to know?" she asked.

"Did he have any problems?" asked Naseem. "Like, was he sick or something?" she continued.

Other students posed questions about the author's personal and professional life. "What about where he lived?" Mauricio inquired. "Maybe it was a messed-up neighborhood."

After compiling a list of exploratory questions, the teacher paired students up to investigate each topic. "You'll have forty-eight hours," she told her students. "Be ready to share what you find out."

Two days later, Nyapal's students were brimming with information. "When people want to share things they know with one another, they usually talk about it. I'd like each of you to write one fact you found out on the strip of yellow paper sitting on your desk." After the students did this, she explained that they'd be using a tea party discussion format—a series of short conversations, each three minutes long, completed with other individual classmates. Every three minutes, Nyapal asked them to move on to another tea party guest to conduct another short conversation, repeating this ten times. In thirty minutes, virtually all of the information the students had found had been shared with the entire class, because newly learned facts were incorporated into subsequent discussions. "Like gossip," Nyapal remarked later. "It spreads fast."

The students were now able to conduct a richer discussion of the meaning of *The Metamorphosis* because they possessed more extensive background knowledge. Students offered theories related to the author's religion ("He was Jewish and he lived in the Jewish ghetto in Prague. Maybe he felt like he didn't belong," explained T. J.), his strained relationship with his father ("They did *not* get along," Brandey offered), his health ("He had tuberculosis," Kristin said), and his unhappy professional life ("Kafka worked in an insurance office and he didn't like his job," Kacia replied). Nyapal revisited their earlier conclusions about symbolism in the story, and they used their newly formed background knowledge to deepen their understanding. Acknowledging that Kafka's central theme was about disrupting the commonplace through the symbolism of a troubling transformation, the students made further connections to their personal and academic lives.

To conclude the lesson, the teacher reread *Beetle Boy*, the picture book she had introduced on the first morning. This time, they immediately saw the obvious connections between this text and Kafka's work. "The little boy's name is Gregory!" exclaimed Dan. "That totally went past me the first time."

Noting the upbeat ending in the children's book, Jose contemplated which ending he would rather see. "I know it's for little kids so you gotta have a happy ending," he began. "But I like Kafka's better. It's dark and all, but it really says something about being hidden away. I think we all feel repulsive sometimes. Kafka just gave it a name."

<h2>Examining Multiple Perspectives</h2>

When Nancy was a youngster, her father shared the secret of how to find the smallest of lost objects. "You've got to get down on the floor, put your ear right next to the ground, and then really look. Even the tiniest object will look like a big tree or mountain sticking up." Sure enough, he was right. The back of an earring, a dropped sewing needle, even a contact lens could usually be found just by changing position to see a new view.

It's amazing what can pop up just by switching viewpoints. In learning, too, we know that ability to look at, and for, multiple perspectives is linked to the development of more complex connections across schemata. As we described in Chapter 1, students who best use their background knowledge are able to recognize similarities and differences across schemata and apply this to new learning. This pattern recognition is essential to analyzing events across time, as is required for historical study and interpretation. Unfortunately, for too many adolescent learners, history is seen as fossilized—a list of dates and names to be memorized, what respected history educator Sam Wineburg calls the "one damned thing after another approach" (2001, 82). He goes on to say that a real threat of this view of a fixed and static history is that "because we more or less know what we are looking for before we enter this past, our encounter is unlikely to change us or cause us to rethink who we are. . . . We are not called upon to stretch our understanding to learn from the past. Instead, we contort the past to fit the predetermined meanings we have already assigned it" (6).

We were fascinated by a study of the ways adolescents used their background knowledge to interpret articles in a newspaper. Students at public and parochial high schools read two contemporary newspaper articles: one concerning allegations of economic abuse by a U.S. corporation on workers in a poor country and the other on school prayer. The researcher found marked differences in the historical events students cited to support their positions on each of the two stories. In nearly all cases, the historical events cited were correct, but the conclusions each group of students reached differed. The author of the study noted, "People do not experience events and situations passively. They actively frame, contemplate, and remember details according to their goals, knowledge, and experience" (Mosborg 2002, 347). If we don't purposefully cause them to examine alternative perspectives, learners are likely to remain in what social psychologists refer to as a construal event—interpreting actions using only one's own perspective.

In order for students to understand a complex event or experience beyond the superficial level, they must seek multiple perspectives. Viewing the same issue from more than one viewpoint casts a dimensionality that cannot exist on the flat plane of isolated facts. What they discover may be wholly surprising or utterly predictable. Regardless, once they understand that issues worth examining require metaphorically putting your ear to the ground, they will see concepts emerge where they had not been previously seen.

U.S. history educators Warren, Memory, and Bolinger (2004) developed a unit of study designed to adopt multiple perspectives about the Vietnam War. They assembled numerous readings for small groups of students to discuss and analyze as possible sources for a paper they would be writing titled "What the United States Should Have Learned from the Vietnam War." These articles included an interview with former defense secretary Robert McNamara, a former Marine lieutenant's letter to an editor, another written by the brother of an American prisoner of war who committed suicide after coming home, and a scholarly article written by a professor of history. Recognizing that reading ability was a form of background knowledge that varied among students, they selected magazine articles using the MAS Ultra—School Index, available through the EBSCOhost library database, because it also reports Lexile scores for each reading. (They note that while this readability measure should not be the only determinant for selecting a text, it did provide them with another dimension of information to ensure that they were differentiating their readings sufficiently.)

The work of Warren, Memory, and Bolinger demonstrates how the use of multiple perspectives can plunge students into a topic not easily addressed by a loose collection of facts. They must not only draw on their background knowledge to understand the readings but also make conscious decisions about how they will apply this information to create a richer schema. By carefully selecting readings that offer opposing, and at times conflicting, perspectives we can help a new dimensionality of understanding emerge.

Multiple Perspectives in Seventh-Grade Science

Fostering multiple perspectives is not always a matter of controversy. However, it does require the ability to look across a broader expanse of information in order to build one's schema. Seventh-grade science teacher Sarah Ryan is encouraging the use of multiple perspectives in order for students to understand life forms in prehistoric times. She begins by distributing artifacts from several geological eras, including a piece of petrified wood, a dragonfly suspended in amber, a fossil of a trilobite, and a dinosaur bone. Most of her students are English learners in the intermediate and early advanced stages of language development, so she spends time on vocabulary instruction, being quick to clarify that "petrified" wood is not scared! She also provides the class with a time line of the geological eras because she understands that the unfamiliar vocabulary is challenging for any student. "See the color I've used on the outside of the container holding your artifact? That matches the color on the geological era time line." Using a much larger version of the time line that stretches down the school's main hallway, Sarah invites the groups to stand on the corresponding locations with their artifacts. "See how far apart in time each of these organisms lived? It's easy to be fooled into thinking that a long time ago is all the same, but when geologists speak about time they are very exact. They use geological eras to describe these times."

After labeling each era they will be learning about—Cambrian, Permian, Triassic, and Jurassic—she explains to her students that they will travel in time to learn about life on Earth during each era. "I want you to see what life was like for creatures during each of those eras," she tells them. "I also want you to understand how it could be very different depending on where that creature fit on the food chain." During the next two class periods, groups rotate among eight stations (two duplicate stations for each era to keep the group size down). Using the laptops Sarah has loaded with information about the era, students learn about what life was like for their organisms. For instance, they learn that the trilobite fossil they held in their hands was likely to be a scavenger that ate dead plants and animals on the bottom of the sea, and curled up to defend itself when attacked. In contrast, the Coelophysis, a carnivorous dinosaur found in New Mexico, is thought to have eaten its own species when the opportunity presented itself.

After learning about each era, each group develops a short collaborative online presentation using VoiceThread. Each group posts images of the era and either records voice comments or writes text comments with each image. Sarah likes using this forum because it allows subsequent groups to add information and ask questions of one another. In this way, the presentations do not remain static, but are enhanced by classmates who can pose questions and respond to one another even across class periods. Although her content lesson is about geological eras, she has created a response format that encourages the use of multiple perspectives to understand both science and one another.

Focusing on Sociopolitical Issues

The broad issues that face a society constitute sociopolitical issues. These are topics that move the reader beyond disruption of commonly held assumptions to look at the role of society and culture as a dimension of an issue. These include power, class, race, privilege, language, and education. Issues of power and class can be very difficult for students to examine because they are so closely anchored to overall identity. For a student who has not experienced loss or gain of power through changing economic fortunes, what one has and does not have is a given. Foss, an eighth-grade English teacher in a predominantly white upper-middle-class suburban community, knew that her students lived what she described as "insulated lives" behind a "membrane" that separated them almost invisibly from the larger world (2002, 394). She wrote:

> Most convey an unspoken belief that they attend a school with outstanding facilities and seemingly endless resources because their families worked hard and earned their place in society. Implied in this philosophy is that other students not so far away geographically find themselves in rundown buildings with leaky roofs and missing books because their families have not worked hard enough to "pull themselves up." (399)

Foss used *To Kill a Mockingbird* (Lee 1960/2002) as a touchstone text to consider the role of privilege in the lives of the main characters. Students read a variety of comparative essays and position pieces by writers like Jonathan Kozol, Erin Gruwell, and Peggy McIntosh to foreground the issue of power and class. Her students began with the more distanced discussions of Lee's characters but over time began to turn inward to examine how privilege influenced their own lives. Foss understood that the first step in getting students to use their background knowledge to adopt a critical literacy stance was to problematize the issue of power and class in the lives of the fictional characters of a novel in order for them to peel the onion for themselves.

As with race and gender, issues of power and privilege are deeply ingrained to the point of being invisible for many students. As Peggy McIntosh explained in her essay on white privilege and power, "I realized I had been taught about racism as something which puts others at a disadvantage, but had been taught to not see one of its corollary aspects, white privilege, which puts me at an advantage" (1988, 1). Understanding power and privilege should not be confined to white students, of course. The goal is to make all students notice how power shades their own background knowledge and influences how they understand and represent information.

Sociopolitical Issues in Ninth-Grade Geography

The students in Christine Quinn's ninth-grade geography class are accustomed to understanding current events within the context of the discipline. Each week, students are required to locate current events that emanate from the focus region of study. Christine explained, "From the first day, I want them to understand that geography isn't just about physical land masses. It's also about understanding the interaction between the people and the landscape. There are historical, political, cultural, and economic influences that change the land. And in turn, the land shapes all these elements."

During their unit of study on Asia, students learned about the unique characteristics of the continent and how the geography of the countries supported and enhanced a sense of isolation. The students examined China and its physical characteristics, including the deserts and mountains that formed a barrier between the Chinese and other civilizations. They also learned about human efforts to increase this isolation, especially the Great Wall of China, and protectionist policies that made it difficult for outsiders to enter. Christine's students learned that thousands of years of isolation worked to China's advantage in some ways, especially in preserving and strengthening cultural and societal norms. In other ways, however, this isolation also limited trade opportunities. Political upheaval during the twentieth century sent the country careening between extreme isolation and a global economy, leaving the country's citizens scrambling to catch up with processes and practices that enhance growth while preserving safety.

During the fall semester, current events regarding food safety in China were also becoming known to the world. In particular, the use of melamine, a nitrogen-rich polymer used in the manufacture of plastic products, had been used for several years in some food and milk products to make it appear as though the protein levels were higher than they really were. It is toxic in animals and humans and affects the urinary system. Mr. Quinn introduced students to several maps, including some that showed the increase in the 1990s in the number of plants in China producing melamine, as well as a chart showing the fall of prices internationally for melamine.

Having built their background knowledge of the topic, Christine assigned partners to locate information about the melamine scandal. Because the story was still evolving, students were able to witness the unfolding of events. Tyrese and Angela located news reports from 2007 regarding the deaths of animals that had been fed pet foods containing high levels of melamine. Using that information, Carter and David found information about the increase of trade during this century that made it possible for pets in other countries to be affected by lax manufacturing controls in

China. Two other partnering teams worked together to find newspaper and magazine reports discussing the suspension of pet food imports from China by the European Union, a region they had formerly studied, to stave off the rash of pet deaths. The work of these and other students extended their peers' background knowledge about the first year when the scandal became apparent.

"I was really looking for this place to hum like a newsroom, and somewhere along the way I came up with the idea of having each class publish a newspaper on their school's wiki (a community web page that allows for collaborative writing using open editing) about melamine in China. That's when I knew we had to become more specialized in our approach," explained Christine. Partners soon evolved into teams covering a particular aspect of the story. Petra and Sonia wrote a piece on the history of trade with China, while Alberto and Mykia created a map showing the topographical and political features of China and the location of its melamine factories. Several partners covered the developing story of milk contamination, infant deaths, and the death sentences of several executives who sold melamine-laced protein powder to manufacturers of baby formula and other food products.

"This really was serendipity," Christine said later. "As teachers we know our content is always changing, but students often get stuck in this false idea that it is static and fixed. That's usually the case with geography. [Students] think that it's just dusty maps and nothing ever changes. This was a chance for them to witness events in real time and see how they used their geographical background knowledge to understand a tragedy that affects so many lives."

Taking Action: The Relationship Between Critical Literacy and Citizenship

Critical literacy skills are vital for citizens of an increasingly "global village" (McLuhan 1962). The instant availability of information and misinformation from all corners of the world requires that readers sort through the barrage of messages, analyzing them for truth, authenticity, and integrity. Critically literate citizens are less vulnerable to propaganda because they understand the role of values and beliefs and consider the sources from which these messages emanate.

The notion of critical literacy is central to a revitalized civics education movement. The Center for Information on Civic Learning and Engagement (CIRCLE) has called for an overhaul of civics education in the United States, noting that the majority of current curricula emphasizes "great American heroes and virtues" but lacks critical analysis of injustice in the American system (Levine and Lopez 2004). Importantly, young people ages fifteen to twenty-five who had been exposed to this approach to civics education were "more trusting," holding an arguably dangerous belief in a complex world, while the small minority (9 percent) who had experienced a curriculum emphasizing critical examination of social injustices such as racism were the most likely to be registered voters. At a time when civic engagement is more important than ever, it would seem that critical analysis of, and within, a democratic system yields a more engaged citizenry. The point should not be lost that the freedom to engage in this discourse is possible because of a democratic system.

Perhaps the best example of civic engagement is when one citizen advocates on behalf of another without regard to personal benefit. *Left for Dead* (Nelson and Scott 2003) describes the efforts of Hunter Scott, an eleven-year-old from Pensacola, Florida, who learned about the World War II disaster suffered by the men of the USS *Indianapolis* while watching the movie *Jaws* with his father in 1996. Hunter researched the court-martial of its captain, who was found guilty of "hazarding" his ship, leading to the deaths of 880 men in shark-infested waters off the coast of Palau. Although the survivors felt their captain was wrongly convicted, they were not able to clear his name. Hunter's interviews with survivors for a history fair project led to a personal campaign to set the record straight. His advocacy on behalf of the now-deceased captain included speaking with politicians, high-ranking Navy officials, and the media. His testimony before the Senate Armed Services Committee, as well as the submission of new evidence uncovered by Hunter, led to the captain's full exoneration in 2000. *Left for Dead* serves as an excellent example of the power of an individual to right a wrong.

Taking action is where background knowledge meets new learning. Students who have learned to foster a critical literacy lens question what they read and ask themselves about the sociopolitical and cultural influences that shape every story. Their move to action is the ultimate transfer of background knowledge because they are applying what they know to a new situation. In addition, the critical literacy lens furthers their own metacognitive awareness as they critically examine how their learning changes over time.

Taking Action in Eighth Grade   The students in Matt Berringer's eighth-grade science class had been learning about the chemistry of living systems and the ways in which it underlies biology. At the same time, these students had also been learning about the challenges of agrarian life for pioneers settling the western United States during the mid-nineteenth century in Corinna Espinoza's social studies class. She had told them about innovative methods used by these people to establish new lives, such as building sod huts in Kansas, employing water diversion techniques for farming in Texas, and using seed varieties that responded well to dry farming conditions.

During lunch one day, the two teachers were bemoaning the amount of lunch waste being thrown away in the school cafeteria. "Too bad we're not as resourceful as the pioneers I've been teaching about in my classes," said Corinna. Corinna remarked on her students' interest in these problem-solving techniques, which inspired the two teachers to develop a unit together. "As we were talking to one another about our content, we realized that we could find a way to expand and apply their background knowledge in order to take action," Corinna explained. "We came up with the idea of starting a composting effort here at our school."

The two teachers met with the entire eighth-grade teaching team to share their ideas and plan next steps. They then took the plan to the students. "We started talking with them about challenges facing our ecosystem today, and Corinna reminded them of the pioneers' challenges 150 years ago," Mr. Berringer stated. "Before long, kids were talking about being 'green pioneers' at the school. That's when we outlined a plan for composting using cafeteria waste."

Thus began a yearlong effort to fund and implement a school composting program. Students learned about efforts by schools around the country to begin similar programs. In conjunction with their teachers, they wrote letters and emails to the principals of these schools. After several received advice on obtaining outside funding to begin the project, other teams of students researched organizations that might be interested. When a team of students received a positive reply from a local civic organization, they learned about developing a funding proposal and presentation. In the meantime, other student teams made it their job to learn all they could about the materials needed to establish and maintain a large compost pile. They had not thought of items such as barrels for the cafeteria, pitchforks and rakes, and gloves for those who would sort vegetable matter from other noncomposting items such as meat and dairy items. Over the course of a few weeks, Mr. Berringer and this team wrote up a price list to propose to the organization. They were delighted when their project funding of fifteen hundred dollars was approved a few weeks later.

By now, the project was taking on a life of its own. Several students formed an education team, with the mission of teaching the school about the composting program and each student's and staff member's role. Representatives presented at meetings of several stakeholders, including the parent-teacher organization, the faculty, and grade-level assemblies. Another team of students, in the company of Corinna, worked with the cafeteria staff to develop a process for collecting and moving food scraps, as well as a schedule of student workers who would be on hand each day to do the work. Mr. Berringer assembled a team of interested students who would collect data to maintain the health of the composting pile and the organisms living within it.

This large-scale program has grown and developed over the years and is now maintained by students who were still in elementary school when the plan to create a composting pile was first developed. A few times a year the compost is available for sale to families at the school, and it sells out within a few hours. "It's amazing to me to look back on the genesis of this program. It's so much a part of the culture of our school that it's hard to imagine what we'd be like without it. And it really did start with two teachers chatting during lunch one day," said Mr. Berringer.

Taking action, like all aspects of teaching critical literacy, requires teacher support. By modeling the tools we use as adults to solve problems, we build our students' capacity to take action themselves. Their engagement with developing solutions makes building their own background knowledge a necessary outcome.

■ What Happened to Jenna?

At the beginning of this chapter, we described an incident that took place in the newsroom where Nancy serves as a high school newspaper advisor. Jenna, a ninth-grade member of the newspaper staff, submitted an article on Mahatma Mohandas Gandhi that contained suspect information. Nancy taught Jenna about seeking sources and using journalistic approaches when developing newspaper articles, but she knew that this wasn't enough.

In the eighteen months or so after this incident occurred, Nancy spent more time with Jenna and the staff on asking the types of questions necessary for understanding and analyzing information. Writers learned to ask the three questions profiled earlier in this chapter—In whose interest? For what purpose? Who benefits?—when researching each news report. Journalists are now required to address each of these when they submit the sources used to develop a report. Jenna was promoted to an editorial staff position in order to gain more experience in asking the kinds of questions necessary for a healthy skeptic. Ultimately, these deeper understandings were the product of ongoing dialogue between teacher and students. The opportunities to engage in debate with fellow learners on a wide range of topics promoted the kind of critical literacy stance they would need as young adults.

■ Conclusion

Critical literacy is not about criticizing; it's about teaching students to think about information rather than accept it at face value. As we build and activate students' background knowledge, we want to be sure that we do so for worthwhile reasons. And what is more worthwhile than compelling students to action, whether it be for someone who has been marginalized, to right a wrong, or to change the world?

New Literacies, Old Standards for Excellence

"Email is for old people, but OK."

Imagine our faces as both of us got up from a meeting with a ninth grader named David. Our jaws dropped no doubt, and Nancy felt like it was time to put 1-800-Assisted-Living on her speed dial. Nothing like a 14-year-old to make one feel 104! We had just met with David to discuss the vlog (video blog) he'd done for an after-school video class he had attended at our school. In the course of discussing it, he'd given us some good suggestions about ways we could improve the class. Doug had just asked David to send him an email with any other ideas he might have when David pronounced email dead, extinct as the poor passenger pigeon.

As adults functioning in a rapidly shifting technology world, we are always on the alert for new ways of making our work easier and better. In fact, we would describe ourselves as being pretty knowledgeable about new technologies. We have a web page (www.fisherandfrey.com), we blog, use social networking sites, we even enroll in educational technology courses at our university. And yet David's casual remark served as a reminder of the difference between new technology and new literacies: tools versus process.

After we swallowed hard and asked what he meant, he explained that he thought email was cumbersome compared with the immediacy of a text message, instant messaging, or a microblog. "I have to go find a computer and log on to my email," he told us. "What if I get a good idea riding home on the bus? It'd be easier to just text."

David's remark showed us he was thinking about process, not tools. For him, an email slowed the process of communication. He was thinking about immediacy. While we were still trying to learn tool after tool, David was giving us a glimpse of where technology was likely to go in the next decade. As noted in the political cartoon in Figure 7.1, communication is changing and we have to consider the implications.

In this chapter, we consider how the new literacies of a digital world allow people to locate, create, and disseminate information at breathtaking speed. Yet this accelerated pace can come at a cost to critical literacy. As it becomes increasingly easier to post to a blog, add to a wiki space, or upload a video, the temporal space that naturally occurred with slower modes has vanished. And with it, lingering over ideas and taking on other viewpoints

Figure 7.1 *The evolution of communication*

have evaporated as well. Have you sent an email in anger that you regretted a moment later? If so, you've been a victim of speed at the expense of critical thinking. For us, background knowledge lies at the nexus of critical literacy and new literacies.

■ Redefining New Literacies

The Internet is arguably the largest collection of knowledge ever assembled by humans. The dream of science fiction writers from decades ago has come true. In terms of the memory and information stored, the Internet is like HAL from *2001: Space Odyssey* (Clark 1968). And like HAL, the Internet has given educators a number of new problems and challenges.

On the positive side, the Internet is the ultimate form of background knowledge because everything is free and easy to find, if you know how to look. While direct experiences clearly build background knowledge, cost and time prevent us from visiting every place we'd like to visit. But that's no longer a problem. The treasures of the earth are available for viewing via the Internet. Just think of all of the virtual museums that are available at your fingertips (see Figure 7.2)!

Marc Prensky, in his 2008 keynote at the National Council of Teachers of English conference, suggested that we have to stop thinking of technology

Name	Site	Highlights
The British Museum	www.britishmuseum.org/	Rosetta stone, ancient Egypt
The Virtual Museum of the City of San Francisco	www.sfmuseum.org/	Photographic and document archives
The Metropolitan Museum of Art	www.metmuseum.org/	Searchable database with items and descriptions
Smithsonian	www.si.edu/	Huge collection with daily highlights
The American Museum of Photography	www.photographymuseum.com/	Guided virtual tour, room by room
Musée du Louvre	www.louvre.fr/	Kaleidoscope view of collection

Figure 7.2 *Sample virtual museums*

in terms of nouns (PowerPoint, YouTube, or Twitter) and instead think in terms of verbs (presenting, sharing and commenting, and communicating). In doing so, he acknowledged the rapidly changing nature of the technology tools we use. And yes, that causes us all stress. We seem to just learn a tool, such as Netscape Navigator, and then it's gone, replaced by the next generation. According to Prensky, that will always be the case with technology. Yet there is something more permanent: the reasons we use the technology. In his words, it's the verbs. In a sense, these are the new literacies, but they are really the old literacies. The tools change, but the purposes remain much the same. When you think about it, it's really related to purposes, and purposes that humans have had for a long time. Take, for example, storing information outside of our bodies. We know that cave art was one way that people met this need. Back in the day, we took notes on paper and stored them in notebooks. Today, we take notes electronically and post them on our blogs and hard drives.

Figure 7.3 contains some of the purposes for which we use technology as well as the tools that currently exist relative to those purposes. By the time this book is published, there will be new tools, but the purposes will likely remain the same. As teachers, we have to think about how we can harness current tools to meet these purposes we have with students.

For example, academic writing instructor Mira Pak (2009) used podcasting as a way to scaffold her students' conceptual understanding in writing. The students in her class were also enrolled in another class that, as a final project assignment, had to create a podcast. Pak helped her students analyze the genre of a podcast, including the parts common to podcasting. By listening to, watching, and analyzing podcasts on familiar topics, the students in

Searching	Collaborating
Google	wikis
Yahoo!	VoiceThread
Lycos	Google Docs
Storing	**Listening**
MP3 players	podcasts
flash drives	iTunes
servers	streaming media
CDs and DVDs	RSS feeds
Communicating	**Producing**
text messaging	Garage Band
Twitter	iMovie
Digg	**Presenting**
video conferencing	PowerPoint
Sharing	Keynote
YouTube	Wimba
blogs	**Networking**
vlogs	MySpace
Flickr	Facebook
	Ning

Figure 7.3 *Technology purposes with current tools*

Pak's class identified key features of podcasting and noted that these were common to other forms of writing. When asked why specific podcasts were easier to follow than others, Pak's students discussed the introductions and how effective they were in helping the listener or watcher know what was coming next. They also discussed the way in which the authors of the podcasts presented information with topic sentences and supporting details. Again, the need is decades old but the technology has changed. And the students in Pak's class felt that "podcasting had helped them learn the curriculum better" (21).

We use a Web-based course management tool (Blackboard) in our high school, which serves a number of purposes for students and teachers. As teachers, we like the quiz feature that provides students with immediate feedback because we know that test format practice (and not test prep a few weeks before the state test) helps students understand the genre and perform better under actual testing conditions (Fisher and Frey 2008; Langer

2001). We also appreciate that this tool provides students with storage and sharing options as well as communication opportunities. Given the electronic discussion boards available via Blackboard, students across periods can share ideas, ask questions, and discuss the content. We were fascinated by a discussion students were having related to genetic mutations. Students from different periods of biology engaged in the conversation, which ranged from asking questions about specific conditions to a debate about preventing disabilities through genetic testing. As you can tell from the following excerpt from the discussion board, background knowledge was important in this conversation:

James: Maybe we should test all pregnant women for genetic problems. I'd want to know if there was a problem with my baby.

Andy: Whoa, not so fast. I think it could be an option, but do you want the government testing and knowing the results? I don't know if I'd want to know.

Maria: Testing should be an option, but that would have to come with counseling.

James: Counseling for what?

Andy: So that people know their options because of the results.

Sarah: If we tested, there'd probably be more abortions.

Andy: Not true. It wouldn't change my mind.

James: I'd just want to know so that I could plan.

Maria: That's my point—people need help with the options if we test for these things.

Brian: But wait, are you saying that people with disabilities then might not be born? Is there something "wrong" with people with disabilities? Maybe it's just part of the human experience. Maybe we shouldn't get so caught up in testing and preventing and just let things be.

■ The Background Knowledge of Reading Comprehension

Anyone who has ever used a search engine knows that typing in a simple phrase results in thousands of hits, some of them relevant and others not. The challenge comes when the irrelevant items are more interesting and take you down an unexpected path. That's not to say that the experience isn't engaging and that you don't learn a lot along the way, but it does mean that you don't have the information you wanted or needed. Pulling yourself back from the tangent requires that you are monitoring your purpose for being there in the first place. Monitoring—a key process in reading comprehension—is as relevant to the screen as it is to print.

However, reading comprehension of print materials—an example of core background knowledge—does not automatically transfer to comprehension of digital text. There is emerging evidence that online reading comprehension is not statistically correlated with students' print reading comprehension, at least as measured on a standardized test (Leu et al. 2005). In other words, while there are probably a number of skills and strategies that are used in both online and offline reading, there are also unique skills demanded by online reading. Given the vast array of information available electronically, teachers have the responsibility of teaching students how to use the Internet. Not only will doing so build their online reading comprehension skills, but the background knowledge students gain will transfer to other situations, even if they have to deploy different skills while reading print.

But, as Leu (2008) pointed out, "the cruelest irony of our times [is this]: Because of public policy failures, those who need our help the most with online reading comprehension actually receive it the least." In too many cases, students who need extensive amounts of background knowledge built and who have had limited access to direct experiences are sitting in class doing worksheets and receiving remedial skill-and-drill instruction. The enormous pressure on schools and districts to raise standardized tests scores often comes at the expense of innovative learning experiences. While basic skills are important, we cannot forget that making progress will require the extensive use of background knowledge, which can be developed as students engage in online learning and comprehension tasks.

As teachers, we have to help students negotiate the Internet in ways that allow them to harness its power as the ultimate background knowledge builder and activator. As such, there are at least three areas that deserve attention, including how to search for information, how to evaluate information, and how to determine relevance of the information.

Searching for Information

Inquiry approaches to education suggest that learning starts with a question. We also know that reading comprehension changes when the reader has a question and is looking for an answer (Taboada and Guthrie 2006). While surfing is common among Internet users, the search always begins with a question or problem. Unlike the TV, we don't just turn on the Internet and see what it will tell us. Thus the first skill required of online comprehension is identifying questions, problems, or issues. Of course print reading can also begin with a question, so there is a convenient spillover effect with teaching this component of online comprehension.

Once students have a question or issue in mind, they have to learn how to search for information. As Leu (2008) noted, "locating information is a circuit breaker skill," meaning that the inability to locate information prevents students from going further with the Internet. Unfortunately, as Leu and his team have discovered, many students are not skilled at searching for information. Some use the .com approach, meaning that they type in the information they're looking for followed by *.com* to see what they get. For example, a group of our students were working on projects related to endangered species when we saw evidence of this faulty process. Here are some examples of what we saw:

- Jay typed in *endangeredspecies.com* and got the website for a plant nursery in Southern California.

- Mariah typed in *endangeredanimals.com* and got a referral site with no specific information.

- Andrew typed in *endangeredturtle.com* to find specific information about sea turtles, but that didn't bring up anything, so he typed in *turtle.net* and opened the site of a software company in London.

In addition to the .com approach, Leu and his colleagues noted that unskilled online readers also used the "click and look" strategy for search engines. In this faulty approach, students type a word or phrase into a search engine and then choose the first result, rarely reading the description. We witnessed our students doing this while seeking information for their research papers on China's one-child policy for our ninth-grade health class. Jessica typed *China one child* into Google and the first return, of 7,270,000 pages, was Wikipedia, which was the only page she ended up using for her paper. While we understand that some of our colleagues are concerned about students' use of Wikipedia, and we certainly don't advocate it as the sole source, we have to confess that we fairly regularly use the site to check information. And, there's evidence that the information is increasingly accurate. For example, Schweitzer's analysis suggested "Wikipedia's coverage of psychological topics was comprehensive" (2008, 81) and that students regularly used this tool for personal and school-related information gathering. So, our issue is not that Jessica used Wikipedia, but that she used *only* it. Jessica was fortunate as the first site provided her with reasonable information.

Mathew wasn't so lucky. He used Ask.com and typed *pro con China child policy* and was provided with a list of choices, one of which was "one child rule," which he selected. That took him to the Responsibility Project, which focuses on teenage mothers abandoning their babies. Knowing that wasn't what he was looking for, he hit the Back button and then went to the next site (about birth control in China), which provided him with a graphic look a various forms of birth control. While it was not on topic, he was interested in this Healthline.com site and spent the rest of the period reading about contraceptives.

Katherine Watkins (2008) created a Google game that she uses to teach students how to refine their search criteria. She helps students use quotation marks to make their searches more exact and reduce the number of items found in a typical search. For example, searching for *African elephant* results in more than 1.5 million pages, whereas searching for *"African elephant"* reduces that number to 745,000. The Google game also introduces students to limiters such as the minus (–) tool, which eliminates specific types of sites. Adding *–tours* to our search of African elephants reduces the number of hits to 502,000. Teachers opposed to Wikipedia can teach students to add *–Wikipedia* to their searches. And finally, students are introduced to the site type function. In the search string, students indicate the type of site they're looking for (e.g., .edu, .gov). Our search for African elephants is further reduced with the function *site:gov* added to the search phrase. The final result is 3,240 sites about African elephants sponsored by government agencies. For more information on search strings and tools for educators, visit www.google.com/educators/all_grades.html.

Searching For and Applying Information in Ninth-Grade Earth Science

In addition to teaching students how to conduct searches, teachers must help students determine which results to use. For example, ninth-grade earth science teacher Nick Baldwin focuses on helping students read the results page to determine if the information they're looking for is available. During his ecology unit, students focused on climate change and how humans are connected with their environment. On one particular day, they were looking for information about the greenhouse effect and specifically about the impact of carbon dioxide on the atmosphere and temperature. Using a data projector, Nick performed his search using the string *"greenhouse effect" site:edu*.

He then explained his thinking for several of the results. For the first site, he said, "This first one sounds interesting: an animated diagram. But that's not what I'm looking for right now. Maybe we'll go back to that later. Right now I'm looking for information about CO_2. The second site doesn't seem to have anything that I need. It's focused on the Northern Hemisphere and the natural greenhouse effect. The third site compares the earth's atmosphere with other planets. Again, interesting, but not what I'm looking for. But here it is on the fourth site. The description discusses the excess greenhouse effect due to raising CO_2. That's the site for me right now."

After the class read and discussed the page he had found, a new question arose. The site introduced the idea of thermal equilibrium. Nick invited his students to work in pairs to find more information about this phenomenon using the class laptops. Before doing so, he reminded them to read the site summaries to determine which sites would help them find the information they were looking for. He said, "Don't just click around, hunting and pecking. Be scientists who know what they're looking for and have precision in their work. You're looking specifically for information about thermal equilibrium in the context of the greenhouse effect and global climate change."

Promoting Search Skills in Your Classroom

Leu and his colleagues identified a number of skills students need to be taught to effectively read search engine results, including the following:

- knowing which portions of a search results page are sponsored, containing commercially placed links, and which are not

- skimming the main results before reading more narrowly

- reading summaries carefully and inferring meaning in the search engine results page to determine the best possible site to visit

- understanding the meaning of URLs in search results (.com, .org, .edu, .net)

- knowing when the first item is not the best item for a question

- monitoring the extent to which a search engine results page matches the information needed

- knowing how to use the history pull-down menu (2008, 344)

Taken together, this list of skills can be used as a needs assessment for students that can guide instruction. When any of the above skills is missing from a student's repertoire, instruction is required. Again, our focus is on building background and the Internet is an excellent tool for doing so. Having said that, if students cannot find information to build their background knowledge, the Internet is reduced to a toy or game and not an educational tool. And once students find information, they have to know how to evaluate that information.

Evaluating Information

Once students know how to search for information, they have to learn to evaluate the credibility of that information. Unfortunately, unskilled online readers rarely evaluate the information they're seeing on the Internet and don't seem to care who created the information placed on a website. Nancy witnessed this when she talked with Jenna about her newspaper article (see Chapter 6). A compelling example of this comes from Leu and his colleagues (2007), who examined seventh graders' analysis of bogus websites. In their study, forty-seven out of fifty-three skilled online readers indicated that a hoax site (Save the Endangered Pacific Northwest Tree Octopus) was real. But even more interesting than the fact that they thought the site provided accurate and reliable information was the students' insistence of its authenticity when told by the researchers that it was a hoax. It seems that students really do believe everything they read when it's found in an electronic environment!

The implications for background knowledge are clear. The Internet has the potential for perpetuating the misconceptions we discussed in Chapter 3. But even worse than that, it has the potential to add new misconceptions to the already complex lives of our students. Accordingly, teachers have to provide intentional instruction on evaluating information found in cyberspace. A critical literacy approach is of value when it comes to evaluating digital information.

Evaluating Information in Sixth-Grade Science

One way we can help students evaluate an electronic source is by teaching them to evaluate the "About Us" or authorship information for the website. For example, Natalie Artiaga requires that her students report this information for each website they want to use. During their investigation of earthquakes, for example, a group of students visited the United States Geological Society's website on earthquakes. Before reading the page, they knew to click on the "About Us" link. There was a great deal of information about the authors, including a map of their locations, a mission statement, and contact information. The top of the page proclaimed, "This web site is provided by the United States Geological Survey's (USGS) Earthquake Hazards Program as part of our effort to reduce earthquake hazard in the United States." Satisfied that this was a credible source, they began to explore the site. Another group, looking for information on the impact of earthquakes, searched *earthquake sounds* and got the site of a stereo store with no "About Us" section and quickly returned to their search results. Another group stumbled on an earthquake relief site for victims of a recent quake in China. They checked the "About Us" page, which provided them with information about a group of citizens raising funds for orphaned children. They noted that the site was probably credible, but not what they were looking for.

When students are first introduced to Web searching, teachers often start with a specific tool that guides the inquiry. A sample website evaluation tool can be found in Figure 7.4. The goal of a tool like this is manyfold. First, we need to build students' background knowledge about websites and searching. Second, we need to help students find relevant and accurate information that they can use. And finally, we have to guide students' use of information such that they are assimilating new information into their stores, or funds, of knowledge.

Evaluating Information in a Middle School Technology Class

Coiro (2005) developed another way to get students to focus on credibility. As part of her teaching, she taught students to ask and answer specific questions when viewing websites (see Figure 7.5). Helping students internalize these questions was a goal of middle school technology teacher Nadine Jamison. Each and every time they visited a website, she reminded them of the questions, which were posted on the wall of her classroom. Over the course of the year, she heard students start to ask themselves and each other these questions as they considered various sources of information. Nadine was pleased, knowing that she had helped her students become informed consumers of information and not victims of scams and misinformation.

Teachers can also use hoax sites to help students understand that the Internet can be misleading. Current hoaxes can be investigated at snopes.com, a very useful site for teachers that debunks myths. Some of our favorite hoax sites for evaluating information include these:

- California's Velcro Crop Under Challenge: www.umbachconsulting.com/miscellany/velcro.html

- Dog Island Free Forever: www.thedogisland.com/

- Buy Dehydrated Water: www.buydehydratedwater.com/

- Yoga Kitty: www.yogakitty.com/

URL: _____

1. Title of website: _____

2. What is the main purpose of this site? _____
    _____

    - Is it selling something?
    - Does it describe a service?
    - Is it an educational site?

3. Who created the site? _____
    _____

    _____

    - What did you learn from the "About Us" section?
    - Is there a contact name, email, or phone number?
    - Was it created by a company, school, government agency, or other?

4. How current is the site (when was it created and when was it updated)? _____
    _____

5. Are links available to other sites? Do they really link? (Try some of them.) _____
    _____

    _____

6. Is this site easily accessible? _____
    - Is the site user-friendly?
    - Is information easy to figure out, follow, find?

7. What did you learn from this site? _____
    _____

    _____

    _____

Figure 7.4 *Website evaluation tool*

Does this information make sense?	⇒	Be skeptical and ask around.
Where else can I look?	⇒	Search the Internet using keywords in quotation marks, or look in a book.
Who created the website and why?	⇒	Explore the "About Us" link with a critical eye.
Who is the author?	⇒	Search the Internet using the author's name in quotation marks.
Who is linking to the site?	⇒	Type "*Link:*" followed by the URL of the website in question into the search box of the Google home page.

Figure 7.5 *Think and check critical reading activity*

Leu and his colleagues identified a number of skills students need to be taught to effectively evaluate websites, including a number of markers of reliability:

- Is this a commercial site?

- Is the author an authoritative source (e.g., professor, scientist, librarian, etc.)?

- Does the website have links that are broken?

- Does the information make sense?

- Does the author include links to other reliable websites?

- Does the website contain numerous typos?

- Does the URL provide any clues to reliability?

- Do the images or videos appear to be altered? (2008, 345)

The first two components of teaching about the Internet to build and activate background knowledge—searching and evaluating—will improve students' online reading comprehension skills. Of course, these skills are also used in print reading and students need to see how they are related. While necessary, these two components will not be sufficient to significantly improve students' access to background knowledge. The third component is critical. As we noted in Chapter 1, there are a lot of students who have a great deal of background knowledge but don't know when to activate it. They aren't sure when specific background knowledge information is useful or how to determine the relevance of that information. The same is true for the vast stores of information available on the Internet. Students must be taught to determine the relevance of the information they find.

Determining the Relevance of Information

As we have noted, the amount of information available on the Internet is unimaginable. Theoretically, there is no end to the Internet. That's why we were humored when we stumbled on the final page of the Internet, which read:

The End of the Internet

Congratulations! This is the last page.

Thank you for visiting the End of the Internet. There are no more links.
You must now turn off your computer
and go do something productive.
Go read a book, for Pete's sake.

Yes, we can spend all day searching the Internet. It provides endless amounts of trivia, some of which is helpful in building background and some of which is not. The challenge is to teach students to determine the relevance of the information they find. And this starts with the question they had when they began their search. Students need to be continually reminded to return to their question, problem, or issue and see if the information they have collected is useful and relevant.

The difference between print and online reading is especially pronounced in this area. It's fairly easy to flip through a book and see if it's too hard or has the information you're looking for. Readers are taught to check headings in an informational text, for example, to see if the information they're looking for is contained in the book. In terms of the Internet, Coiro and Dobler suggest an important strategy that online readers must develop:

> Given their prior knowledge and the information available, readers actively evaluate the relevance of the choice: Does this choice bring me closer or further away from my goal? Is this a likely and appropriate place for the information I need? Should I move to a deeper level, select a related topic, revert back to an earlier location, or start all over again? (2007, 236)

According to Coiro and Dobler, readers use a recursive system while searching for and locating texts within the Internet. Following are the four components of that system, which is interactive as well as recursive:

- *Plan:* Set a purpose and develop and mental plan.

- *Predict:* Predict where a reading choice may lead.

- *Monitor:* Monitor after making a choice.

- *Evaluate:* Evaluate the relevance of the choice. (235)

*Evaluating
Information in
Eleventh-Grade
English*
The challenge for teachers is to design instruction such that students develop each of these skills. Eleventh-grade English teacher Melody Myers is attempting this as she engages her students in WebQuests on the Harlem Renaissance (Dodge 1995). There are hundreds of WebQuests available at www.webquest.org/index.php. The task for this particular WebQuest reads:

> You and your group members are students at DeWitt Clinton High School, New York, during the Harlem Renaissance Movement. Each member of your group is a writer for the school's publication *The Magpie.* You have been assigned to explore the streets of Harlem in search of local artists. Once you have found an artist, it is your job to interview him/her, in order to find out his/her background history, and then critique his/her work. After your experiences with the artist each of you have chosen, the four members of your group will work together in order to fill the pages of the "Local Arts and Entertainment Review" section of *The Magpie.* (questgarden.com/55/56/7/071208171131/task.htm)

Melody reminds her students that they will find lots of interesting information on the Internet about the Harlem Renaissance, but that it won't all be relevant. She reminds her students to bookmark interesting but irrelevant pages so that they can return to them later. Melody knows that her students understand relevance but, like all of us, get caught up in the tidbits of information that are everywhere. She has found that the bookmark feature, and a little free time on the computer, ensures that students remain focused on the task at hand. Other teachers provide students a log for keeping track of interesting websites that they'll revisit on their own time, and still other teachers allow students a specific number of free prints so that they can read the pages later, when they're not engaged in their productive group work.

■ Old Literacy, Critical Literacy, New Literacy . . .

Thus far in this chapter, we have discussed the background knowledge needed to extract and evaluate information using digital sources. These are the verbs associated with receptive literacy—searching, comprehending, evaluating, as so on. But the truly exciting explosion of Web 2.0—the term used to describe the ways in which a person acts upon and creates digital information—has provided educators with a new array of possibilities for students to utilize their background knowledge. These are the collaborative and interactive means for sharing, presenting, and networking. Some are print based, but many are not. And they require an even higher level of background knowledge.

It seems like every week there is a new tool for teachers to use to encourage collaboration among their students. We have discussed several of them in this book—VoiceThread, wikis, and discussion boards, to name a few. These tools provide students an opportunity to meet yet another need: to interact with others. But we're not talking about social networking sites. Instead, we're thinking about the ways in which students can engage in productive group work using technology.

We are particularly interested in the work being done by Leu and his colleagues on Internet reciprocal teaching. Most teachers are familiar with reciprocal teaching and the conversations students have while reading printed texts. In general, students summarize, predict, question, and clarify with each other as they engage in reading (Palincsar 1987). In addition to the "regular" reading students do with the Internet, they also use the four components of reciprocal teaching to analyze the accuracy of specific sites. They might have conversations based on the following questions:

- *Predict:* Do you think your site is a reliable source of information?

- *Question:* How do you know that a website has accurate information?

- *Clarify:* How do you go about checking on the validity of websites?

- *Summarize:* Which strategies were most useful? Which were not?

Of course students need to be taught how to engage in Internet reciprocal teaching, and Leu and his colleagues provide a template for implementation (www.newliteracies.uconn.edu/carnegie/documents/IRT.pdf). Interestingly, there are a number of ways to use this protocol, such as for

- reading between two web pages (a home page and one linked web page)

- reading within multiple web pages bound to one website

- reading within a search engine

- reading the entire Web

- reading (and writing) online messages

■ Conclusion

Adolescents often exhibit an overconfidence in their own abilities to locate and understand information on the Internet. Many believe that simple search techniques such as typing in a keyword followed by a domain will yield the information they need. Yet this can expose them to misleading or inaccurate information. Without a critical literacy lens that compels the reader to ask questions about the source—especially the interests, purpose, and benefits to the individual or group—students like Jenna, whose story we told in Chapter 6, remain vulnerable.

These questions are valid for both print and digital resources and can foster metacognitive awareness about students' own learning. More importantly, a critical literacy lens causes students to closely examine their own background knowledge, acquired through prior experiences as well as classroom learning, to understand how their perceptions of the world are similar to and different from other people's. Ultimately, background knowledge isn't private, and it doesn't exist in a vacuum, untouched by other influences. Background knowledge is shared, shaped, and changed through public engagement with ideas and people. A digital world has expanded the opportunities for learners to do just that, but it has also decreased the time they have to consider whether an idea was worth adopting or not. A critical literacy approach to new literacies buys back some of that time and causes students to use their background knowledge to analyze new information.

Building and Activating Background Knowledge Is Our Job

CLEARLY, THE 1990S WERE THE DECADE of the brain. More information was collected during that decade than had been assembled in the century before. And information about the human brain continues to be amassed at an astounding rate. Like many educators, we are both intrigued with, and suspicious about, the findings of neuroscientists and wonder if *"unequivocal* educational implications" can be drawn from neuroscience (Sternberg 2008, 418). Yet we are curious and wonder if neuroscience might confirm and extend our understanding of the most amazing machine ever created—the human brain. In wondering about the application of neuroscience to education, Willingham said, "I don't understand what my computer hardware is doing as I type this reply, but if I did, that knowledge would not change how I typed or what I wrote" (2008, 422). But Willingham understands something more important about his computer's hard drive, namely the best ways to store and retrieve information. And that's our goal here.

As teachers, we are all brain workers. As brain workers, we attempt to influence that which is stored inside a student's head and to teach in ways that keep our student's head and heart connected. That is, we want information and intellect to always filter through our teachings about humanity—social justice, ethics, compassion, and all the rest along those lines. Or put in terms of accessing knowledge, we hope to provide students with experiences that allow them to draw upon that which is stored in their memory banks so that they can think new thoughts, ask new questions, and solve new problems—problems we might not even know exist yet. And as you might have guessed, each of these abilities rests on background knowledge.

As teachers—brain workers—our job is not to simply fill students' heads with facts. This is where we take exception with the idea of core knowledge, especially core knowledge that privileges one group over another and that is filled with basic skills (Squire 1988; Tchudi 1988). While we agree with Hirsch's claim that "particular content which is learned in school is far less important than acquiring the formal tools which will enable a person to learn future content" (1996, 218), we do not see the answer to this being a collection of facts in third grade, fourth grade, and so on (e.g., Hirsch 2002).

Instead, we see a laserlike focus on assessing, building, and activating background knowledge as teaching students how to think. It's the culture of thought that we're after. Like Brown (1991), we want to be sure that our students have the necessary content knowledge to think critically and creatively, to solve problems, exercise judgment, and learn throughout their lifetimes. In other words, we don't want to spend our days trying to cram little bits of information into students' heads. Instead, we want to ensure that students have information, content, at their fingertips or tongue-tips that they can use to think, understand, and express themselves.

■ Creating Habits

We think that focusing on background knowledge facilitates the habits of mind that Costa and Kallick (2009) have shared with the world. Each of the following sixteen habits is influenced by students' background knowledge (www.habits-of-mind.net/whatare.htm):

- persisting

- thinking and communicating with clarity and precision

- managing impulsivity

- gathering data through all senses

- listening with understanding and empathy

- creating, imagining, innovating

- thinking flexibly

- responding with wonderment and awe

- thinking about thinking (metacognition)

- taking responsible risks

- striving for accuracy

- finding humor

- questioning and posing problems

- thinking interdependently

- applying past knowledge to new situations

- remaining open to continuous learning

As an interesting exercise, you might consider investigating the role that background knowledge plays in one or more of these habits. In one of our teacher meetings, we had a conversation about the role of background knowledge in thinking flexibly. As a group, we came to understand that flexible thinking requires that students mobilize a lot of different information and look for connections between and among ideas. To develop the habit of flexible thinking, students need experiences with examining point of view, considering several sources at once, and applying different problem-solving strategies; interestingly we hypothesized that they also need to learn to trust their intuition.

The background knowledge students need for each of the components of flexible thinking we identified is not a set of basic skills and factoids. Instead, it is experience with accessing and manipulating information. And we can complete this level of analysis with any of the habits of mind. Our experience has taught us that building background ensures that students develop these habits and ways of thinking.

■ Background Knowledge Is a Process

One of the major points we hope you gained from this book is that background knowledge is not a collection of facts that students should memorize. Further, we hope that we have communicated our belief that background knowledge should not be relegated to a set of strategies that are implemented intermittently throughout the day or week. Instead, we see assessing, building, and activating background knowledge as a process that is at the heart of every interaction we have with students. To review, we have to have a fairly good idea of the enduring understandings students need. We also have to know what students already know. Assessments of background knowledge allow us to unearth students' understandings and identify misconceptions, oversimplifications, and overgeneralizations. In addition, we have to have sophisticated instructional routines that allow us to build and activate students' background knowledge. Again, this is not about a collection of facts that students need to memorize but information that students should be able to use to learn new things.

As we think about our own teaching, we ask ourselves questions about what we want to accomplish and what we need to do to get there. As a starting place, you might want to ask yourself the following questions:

- Have I identified enduring understandings for this lesson, topic, or unit?

- Have I determined core versus incidental background knowledge for this topic?

- Have I assessed students such that I recognize their current understandings?

- Have I established a purpose that makes learning relevant for students?

- Have I modeled and demonstrated my own understanding before requiring students to complete learning tasks?

- Have I focused on students' background knowledge that moves beyond facts and isolated skills?

- Have I provided students with wide reading opportunities to facilitate students' background knowledge gains?

- Have I planned live and virtual experiences to build students' background knowledge?

- Do I regularly activate students' background knowledge?

- Do I remind students that background knowledge is critical to understanding?

■ From Where We Began

Rescue the next generation? We started this book by stating that this might be a bit melodramatic. We hope that as you arrive at the end of this book, you might be convinced that it's not such an overstatement after all.

A Study Guide for
Background Knowledge

This study guide is intended to support your understanding of the concepts presented in *Background Knowledge: The Missing Piece of the Comprehension Puzzle*, by Douglas Fisher and Nancy Frey. You can use this study guide as you finish each chapter or after you complete the whole book. Prompts and questions are intended to promote personal reflection but could also be used to foster small-group discussions between colleagues.

■ Chapter 1
The Missing Piece of the Comprehension Puzzle

1. Discuss a time when a lack of background knowledge made it difficult to learn something new. For example, you may have needed to set up a new component to your entertainment system, or you may have taken a few lessons on using a new computer program. How did your lack of background knowledge impede your learning? How did you build your background knowledge so you could be successful?

2. When matching text to students, teachers typically consider several factors, including the readability level of the text and the reading ability of the students. However, they rarely consider background knowledge in anything more than a superficial way. Can you recall times when a student's background knowledge positively affected his ability to read a book that otherwise would have been considered too difficult? What about the reverse situation—a time when the lack of background knowledge interfered with the comprehension of an otherwise understandable text?

3. Bardeen and Lederman (1998) found that physics principles govern other scientific concepts, such as osmosis in biology and molecular structures in chemistry. Others disagree. Sadler and Tai (2007) performed a large-scale study of eight thousand college students and found that sequence did not predict grades in introductory science courses, but the number of years of high school mathematics did. How might background knowledge play a key role in both of these otherwise contradictory findings?

4. In what ways do you foster transfer (application of new learning to novel situations) in your teaching? What conditions make it more successful? Under what circumstances does transfer break down?

5. How has the availability of vast amounts of background knowledge available on the Internet influenced learners in your classes? What do you see as the positive aspects as well as the possible drawbacks to such availability?

6. Vocabulary and background knowledge are intertwined. How do you use vocabulary knowledge as a way of determining background knowledge? How does the degree of vocabulary knowledge serve as a proxy for background?

7. Background knowledge is one thing; retrieval of that information is another. What do your students seem to remember best?

Chapter 2

Placing Background Knowledge in Daily Teaching

1. How is teaching different from telling?

2. How does a gradual release of responsibility model of instruction contribute to building background knowledge? What areas of this instructional design process do you do best? What areas would you like to improve?

3. In what ways do students benefit from your background knowledge? How can you help students benefit from your background knowledge?

4. Analyze a unit you recently taught. What background knowledge did your students need in order to do well? How did you build the prerequisite background knowledge for those who lacked it?

5. What resources are available at your school for building your students' background knowledge?

Chapter 3

Teacher as Archaeologist: Assessing Background Knowledge

1. We used the analogy of an archeologist to explain the role of assessment in teaching. What metaphors would you use to describe it?

2. We described four determinants for differentiating between core and incidental knowledge: *representation* (Is it essential?), *transmission* (Can it be easily explained, or must it be taught?), *transferability* (Will it be used for future understanding?), and *endurance* (What will be remembered after the details are forgotten?). Use these four criteria to discuss examples of core and incidental background knowledge in your discipline.

3. What are the common misconceptions your students bring to your class? How do these misconceptions impede learning?

4. Describe your experiences with anticipation guides and opinionnaires. Why would it be helpful to include common misconceptions about a topic on such an instrument?

5. Why is it necessary to ask for a rationale or explanation from the student when administering an anticipation guide or opinionnaire?

6. How could you incorporate a cloze procedure into your classroom practice? What would you expect it to tell you about your students' background knowledge?

7. Which units of study do your students find the most interesting? Which are the least popular? Discuss how you might use an interest survey for the purposes of designing curriculum.

Chapter 4

Activating What Students Know: Teaching That Unearths and Upends Students' Understandings

1. Think about a time when you had to learn something new, but it seemed to be without a clear purpose. What happens to learning when there is a lack of purpose?

2. How would you expect your students to describe the purpose of their content learning? Beyond compliance issues, in what ways do you spur their learning?

3. Lessons that cause students to consider an issue from more than one perspective can be effective in activating background knowledge. How can you utilize multiple perspectives in your course?

4. Quick writes are commonly used to activate background knowledge, but they are rarely used beyond the immediate learning event. How could you return to previously constructed quick writes to build metacognitive awareness? What benefits do you see in doing so?

5. Partner conversations are a vital part of learning, but they can be difficult for novice teachers to manage. What are the most common challenges you see for new teachers in developing instructional routines for partner talk? How would you explain the necessity of peer conversations for activating background knowledge? What instructional routines do you share with your colleagues who are trying to implement collaborative learning to make the management of peer conversations run more smoothly?

6. Have you used checklists in your classroom? If so, what were the successes? Were there errors that you changed the next time you used the checklist?

7. Construct a language frame collaboratively in one or more content areas. How could you use the language frame in your teaching?

Chapter 5

Quickening the Pace of Students' Background Knowledge Acquisition

1. Consider the students in your classroom or school who are English learners. What background knowledge do they need in your class in order to succeed? What background knowledge do they possess but rarely have the opportunity to display?

2. What are the differences between direct and indirect learning experiences for building background knowledge? What examples of both occur in your class?

3. How do you capitalize on field trips and other experiential learning activities back in the classroom?

4. What are your experiences with modeling using a think-aloud approach? If you don't have much experience at this, what do you think would help you?

5. Compare the reading lives of two students in your class—one who seems to read all the time and another who is almost never seen with a book or magazine. How does this differential level of exposure to reading play out in your classroom?

6. Would your students describe you as a reader? What evidence would they use to support their claims?

7. Pilgreen (2000) says that effective SSR (sustained silent reading) programs do not feature an accountability requirement (book report, test, number of pages read, etc.). This is a controversial stand. What's your opinion? Why?

8. What are the most useful graphic organizers in your content area? How do students utilize them once they have completed these tools? How do you build their capacity to select their own graphic organizers to visually represent information?

Chapter 6
Critical Literacy: Helping Students Get Beyond the Sift-and-Surf Mode to Deep Synthesis of Texts

1. What examples have you experienced with students who have a naïve belief about the veracity of information found on the Internet? How have you helped them when this has occurred?

2. In this chapter, we said, "As teachers of adolescents and citizens of the world, we are concerned that the emphasis on declarative knowledge (facts) has pushed conditional knowledge (knowing when and why to apply information) to the side." Please react to this statement. Do you agree or disagree?

3. The Tasmania (New Zealand) Department of Education (2006) uses a simple but powerful framework for provoking a critical literacy stance: *In whose interest? For what purpose? Who benefits?* How might you apply one or more of these ideas in your content area?

4. What experiences or readings have you used to disrupt the commonplace in your content area? What were the reactions of students? Families?

5. Respected history educator Sam Wineburg calls the traditional history curriculum the "one damned thing after another approach" (2002). What gets lost when students view history as an unending list of facts to memorize? How can this put them in peril?

6. What are the challenges and cautions in utilizing a critical literacy approach in your classroom? How is this balanced against community expectations and state standards?

7. Taking a critical literacy approach in the absence of background knowledge is foolhardy. How can a lack of background knowledge hurt a student?

Chapter 7

New Literacies, Old Standards for Excellence

1. Discuss the evolution of technology as it moves from an emphasis on tools to a focus on processes. How might this shift in perspectives shape the technology policies of your classroom, school, and district?

2. What do you believe should be the role of teaching about new literacy genres such as podcasting, blogs, and so on? Is this critical to background knowledge? Why or why not?

3. Research is the backbone of formal background building, and searching for such information is more complex in a digital world. What correlation do you see between traditional research instruction and digital research instruction? What methods should be retained, and what needs to be added or revised?

4. What tips do you teach your students about how to discern between spurious information and facts that come from reliable sources? What are the inherent difficulties of doing so in your content area? What common errors do your students make?

5. What is the relationship between critical literacy and new literacies? How could you teach both together?

6. Background knowledge isn't just used through a receptive process; students use it expressively when they speak and write. How could you apply an instructional routine like Internet reciprocal teaching, as described by Don Leu and his colleagues (2006), to promote expressive uses of background knowledge?

Chapter 8

Building and Activating Background Knowledge Is Our Job

1. Choose a unit of study you will be teaching in the near future and analyze it using these questions:

   • Have I identified enduring understandings for this lesson, topic, or unit?

   • Have I determined core versus incidental background knowledge for this topic?

   • Have I assessed students such that I recognize their current understandings?

   • Have I established a purpose that makes learning relevant for students?

- Have I modeled and demonstrated my own understanding before requiring students to complete learning tasks?

- Have I focused on students' background knowledge that moves beyond facts and isolated skills?

- Have I provided students with wide reading opportunities to facilitate their background knowledge gains?

- Have I planned live and virtual experiences to build students' background knowledge?

- Do I regularly activate students' background knowledge?

- Do I remind students that background knowledge is critical to understanding?

2. How can schoolwide conversations contribute to a better understanding of students' background knowledge?

3. What currently gathered assessment information can you as an individual teacher use to gain a better understanding of students' background knowledge?

4. In what ways can educators partner with families to build, activate, and utilize background knowledge?

References

BARDEEN, M. G., AND L. M. LEDERMAN. 1998. "Coherence in Science Education." *Science* 281: 178–79.

CASTEK, J., D. J. LEU JR., J. COIRO, D. HARTMAN, AND L. A. HENRY. 2006. "The Changing Nature of Online Reading Comprehension: Examining Effects of Internet Reciprocal Teaching on Adolescents' Acquisition of New Literacies and Content Knowledge in Science." Research paper and poster presented at the 51st annual International Reading Association Conference. Chicago, IL.

PILGREEN, J. L. 2000. *The SSR Handbook: How to Organize and Manage a Sustained Silent Reading Program*. Portsmouth, NH: Heinemann.

SADLER, P. M., AND R. H. TAI. 2007. "The Two High School Pillars Supporting College Science." *Science* 317: 457–58.

TASMANIA DEPARTMENT OF EDUCATION. 2006. *English Learning Area: Critical Literacy*. Retrieved May 31, 2007, from wwwfp.education.tas.gov.au/English/critlit.htm.

WINEBURG, S. 2002. *Historical Thinking and Other Unnatural Acts: Charting the Future of Teaching the Past*. Philadelphia: Temple University Press.

References

Chapter 1

ALEXANDER, P.A., J. M. KULIKOWICH, AND S. K. SCHULZE. 1994. "How Subject-Matter Knowledge Affects Recall and Interest." *American Educational Research Journal* 31: 313–37.

ATKINSON, R. K., R. CATRAMBONE, AND M. M. MERRILL. 2003. "Aiding Transfer in Statistics: Examining the Use of Conceptually Oriented Equations and Elaborations During Subgoal Learning." *Journal of Educational Psychology* 95: 762–73.

BARD, A. S., AND M. G. BARD. 2002. *The Complete Idiot's Guide to Understanding the Brain*. New York: Alpha Books.

BARDEEN, M. G., AND L. M. LEDERMAN. 1998. "Coherence in Science Education." *Science* 281: 178–79.

BARTLETT, F. C. 1932. *Remembering*. Cambridge: Cambridge University Press.

BROWN, R. 1991. *Schools of Thought: How the Politics of Literacy Shape Thinking in the Classroom*. San Francisco: Jossey-Bass.

CATRAMBONE, R. 1995. "Aiding Subgoal Learning: Effects on Transfer." *Journal of Educational Psychology* 87: 5–17.

COIRO, J., AND E. DOBLER. 2007. "Exploring the Online Reading Comprehension Strategies Used by Sixth-Grade Skilled Readers to Search for and Locate Information on the Internet." *Reading Research Quarterly* 42: 214–57.

COSTA, A. L., AND B. KALLICK. 2009. *Leading and Learning with Habits of Mind: Sixteen Essential Characteristics for Success*. Alexandria, VA: Association for Supervision and Curriculum Development.

COWAN, N. 1998. "Visual and Auditory Working Memory." *Trends in Cognitive Sciences* 2: 77–78.

CRAIN-THORESON, C., M. Z. LIPPMAN, AND D. McCLENDON-MAGNUSON. 2004. "Windows on Comprehension: Reading Comprehension Processes as Revealed by Two Think-Aloud Procedures." *Journal of Educational Psychology* 89: 579–91.

DISESSA, A. A. 1993. "Toward an Epistemology of Physics." *Cognition and Instruction* 10: 105–225.

FISHER, D., N. FREY, AND D. LAPP. 2009. *In a Reading State of Mind: Brain Research, Teacher Modeling, and Comprehension Instruction*. Newark, DE: International Reading Association.

GARCÍA, G. E. 1991. "Factors Influencing the English Reading Test Performance of Spanish-Speaking Hispanic Children." *Reading Research Quarterly* 26: 371–92.

GOLDBERG, S. 2007. *Clinical Neuroanatomy Made Ridiculously Simple*. 3d ed. Miami: MedMaster.

GOLDMAN, S. R., AND J. A. RAKESTRAW. 2000. "Structural Aspects of Constructing Meaning from Text." In *Handbook of Reading Research*, vol. III, ed. M. Kamil, P. B. Mosenthal, P. D. Pearson, and R. Barr, 311–36. Mahwah, NJ: Lawrence Erlbaum.

GONZÁLEZ, N., L. MOLL, L., AND C. AMANTI. 2005. *Funds of Knowledge: Theorizing Practices in Households, Communities, and Classrooms*. Mahwah, NJ: Lawrence Erlbaum.

GUTHRIE, J. T., AND A. WIGFIELD. 2000. "Engagement and Motivation in Reading." In *Handbook of Reading Research*, vol. III, ed. M. L. Kamil and P. B. Mosenthal, 403–22. Mahwah, NJ: Lawrence Erlbaum.

HAMMADOU, J. 1991. "Interrelationships Among Prior Knowledge, Inference, and Language Proficiency in Foreign Language Reading." *The Modern Language Journal* 75: 27–39.

HARLAAR, N., M. E. HAYIOU-THOMAS, P. S. DALE, AND R. PLOMIN. 2008. "Why Do Preschool Abilities Correlate with Later Reading? A Twin Study." *Journal of Speech, Language, and Hearing Research* 51 (3): 688–705.

HART, B., AND T. R. RISLEY. 1995. *Meaningful Differences in the Everyday Experiences of Young American Children*. Baltimore: Paul H. Brookes.

HEBB, D. 1949. *The Organization of Behavior*. New York: Wiley.

HOWARD, P. J. 2006. *The Owner's Manual for the Brain: Everyday Applications from Mind-Brain Research*. 3d ed. Austin, TX: Bard.

LANGER, J. A. 1984. "Examining Background Knowledge and Text Comprehension." *Reading Research Quarterly* 14: 468–81.

LEDOUX, J. 2002. *Synaptic Self.* New York: Viking.

MARTIN, M.O., I. V. S. MULLIS, E. J. GONZALEZ, AND S. J. CHROSTOWSKI. 2004. *TIMSS 2003 International Science Report: Findings from IEA's Trends in International Mathematics and Science Study at the Fourth and Eighth Grades.* Chestnut Hill, MA: TIMSS and PIRLS International Study Center, Boston College.

MARZANO, R. J. 2004. *Building Background Knowledge for Academic Achievement: Research on What Works in Schools.* Alexandria, VA: Association for Supervision and Curriculum Development.

McKOON, G., AND R. RATCLIFF. 1992. "Inference During Reading." *Psychological Review* 99: 440–66.

McVEE, M. B., K. DUNSMORE, AND J. R. GAVELEK. 2005. "Schema Theory Revisited." *Review of Educational Research* 75: 531–66.

MEDINA, J. 2008. *Brain Rules: 12 Principles for Surviving and Thriving at Work, Home, and School.* Seattle: Pear.

MILLER, G. A. 1956. "The Magical Number Seven, Plus or Minus Two: Some Limits on Our Capacity for Processing Information." *Psychological Review* 63: 81–97.

MINNINGER, J. 1984. *Total Recall: How to Boost Your Memory Power.* Emmaus, PA: Rodale.

MYHILL, D. 2005. "Testing Times: The Impact of Prior Knowledge on Written Genres Produced in Examination Settings." *Assessment in Education* 12: 289–300.

NATIONAL READING PANEL. 2000. *Teaching Children to Read: An Evidence-Based Assessment of the Scientific Research Literature on Reading and Its Implications for Reading Instruction.* Washington, DC: National Institute of Child Health and Human Development.

NATIONAL RESEARCH COUNCIL. 2000. *How People Learn: Brain, Mind, Experience, and School.* Committee on Developments in the Science of Learning, J. D. Bransford, A. L. Brown, and R. Cocking (eds.), Commission on Behavioral and Social Sciences and Education. Washington, DC: National Academy Press.

PARIS, S. G., B. A. WASIK, AND J. C. TURNER. 1991. "The Development of Strategic Readers." In *Handbook of Reading Research*, vol. II, ed. R. Barr,

M. L. Kamil, P. Mosenthal, and P. D. Pearson, 609–40. Mahwah, NJ: Lawrence Erlbaum.

RAND READING STUDY GROUP. 2002. *Reading for Understanding: Toward an R&D Program in Reading Comprehension.* Office of Educational Research and Improvement. Santa Monica, CA: RAND.

ROBINSON, D. H. 1998. "Graphic Organizers as Aids to Text Learning." *Reading Research and Instruction* 37: 85–105.

RUMELHART, D. E. 1984. "Schemata and the Cognitive System." In *Handbook of Social Cognition*, ed. R. S. Wyer and T. K. Srull, 161–88. Hillsdale, NJ: Lawrence Erlbaum.

SADLER, P. M., AND R. H. TAI. 2007. "The Two High School Pillars Supporting College Science." *Science* 317: 457–58.

SAMUELS, S. J. 2002. "Reading Fluency: Its Development and Assessment." *What Research Has to Say About Reading Instruction*, 3d ed., ed. A. E. Farstrup and S. J. Samuels, 163–88. Newark, DE: International Reading Association.

SCHACTER, D. L. 1999. "The Seven Sins of Memory: Insights from Psychology and Cognitive Neuroscience." *American Psychologist* 54 (3): 182–203.

SHADMEHR, R., AND H. H. HOLCOMB. 1997. "Neural Correlates of Motor Memory Consolidation." *Science* 277: 821–25.

STAHL, S. A., AND M. M. FAIRBANKS. 1986. "The Effects of Vocabulary Instruction: A Model-Based Meta-analysis." *Review of Educational Research* 56 (1): 72–110.

WAGNER, J. F. 2003. "Transfer in Pieces." *Cognition and Instruction* 24: 1–71.

WILLIAMS, R. L., AND A. C. EGGERT. 2002. "Notetaking Predictors of Test Performance." *Teaching of Psychology* 29: 234–37.

WOLFE, M. B. W., AND S. R. GOLDMAN. 2005. "Relations Between Adolescents' Text Processing and Reasoning." *Cognition and Instruction* 23: 467–502.

WOLFE, P. 2001. *Brain Matters: Translating Research into Classroom Practice.* Alexandria, VA: Association for Supervision and Curriculum Development.

YATES, F. A. 1966. *The Art of Memory.* New York: Penguin.

ZWIERS, J. 2007. "Teacher Practices and Perspectives for Developing Academic Language." *International Journal of Applied Linguistics* 17 (1): 93–116.

■ Chapter 2

APPLEBY, J., A. BRINKLEY, A. S. BROUSSARD, J. M. MCPHERSON, AND D. A. RITCHIE. 2003. *The American Republic to 1877.* New York: Glencoe McGraw-Hill.

FISHER, D., AND N. FREY. 2008. *Better Learning Through Structured Teaching: A Framework for the Gradual Release of Responsibility.* Alexandria, VA: Association for Curriculum Supervision and Development.

FREEDMAN, R. 2000. *Give Me Liberty! The Story of the Declaration of Independence.* New York: Holiday House.

PEARSON, P. D., AND M. C. GALLAGHER. 1983. "The Instruction of Reading Comprehension." *Contemporary Educational Psychology* 8: 317–44.

VYGOTSKY, L. S. 1978. *Mind in Society.* Ed. M. Cole, V. John-Steiner, S. Scribner, and E. Souberman. Cambridge, MA: Harvard University Press.

■ Chapter 3

CROSS, D. R., AND S. PARIS. 1988. "Developmental and Instructional Analyses of Children's Metacognition and Reading Comprehension." *Journal of Educational Psychology* 80 (2): 131–42.

DANIELS, H. 2002. *Literature Circles: Voice and Change in Book Clubs and Reading Groups.* York, ME: Stenhouse.

DECI, E. L., AND R. M. RYAN. 1985. *Intrinsic Motivation and Self-Determination in Human Behavior.* New York: Plenum.

ELSTER, D. 2007. "Student Interests: The German and Austrian ROSE Survey." *Journal of Biological Education* 42 (1): 5–11.

ERICSSON, K. A., AND N. CHARNESS. 1994. "Expert Performance: Its Structure and Acquisition." *American Psychologist* 49: 725–47.

FISHER, D., W. G. BROZO, N. FREY, AND G. IVEY. 2007. *50 Content Area Strategies for Adolescent Literacy.* Upper Saddle River, NJ: Pearson Merrill Prentice Hall.

FISHER, D., N. FREY, AND D. LAPP. 2008. "Shared Readings, Modeling Comprehension, Vocabulary, Text Structures, and Text Features for Older Readers." *The Reading Teacher* 61: 548–56.

FOUNTAS, I. C., AND G. S. PINNELL. 2007. *Benchmark Assessment System.* Portsmouth, NH: Heinemann.

HAEDERLE, MICHAEL. 2009. "Mystery of Ancient Pueblo Jars Is Solved." *New York Times* February 4: A14.

LESLIE, L., AND J. S. CALDWELL. 2005. *Qualitative Reading Inventory—4.* Boston: Pearson Allyn and Bacon.

NATIONAL RESEARCH COUNCIL. 2000. *How People Learn: Brain, Mind, Experience, and School.* Committee on Developments in the Science of Learning, J. D. Bransford, A. L. Brown, and R. Cocking (eds.), Commission on Behavioral and Social Sciences and Education. Washington, DC: National Academy Press.

———. 2001. *Knowing What Students Know: The Science and Design of Educational Assessment.* Committee on the Foundations of Assessment, J. W. Pellegrino, N. Chudowsky, and R. Glaser (eds.), Center for Education. Washington, DC: National Academy Press.

POE, E. A. 1846/2002. *Edgar Allan Poe: Complete Tales and Poems.* Edison, NJ: Castle.

REMY, R. C., J. J. PATRICK, D. C. SAFFELL, AND G. E. CLAYON. 2003. *Civics Today: Citizenship, Economics, and You.* New York: Glencoe McGraw-Hill.

SCHMITT, M. C. 1990. "A Questionnaire to Measure Children's Awareness of Strategic Reading Processes." *The Reading Teacher* 43: 454–61.

SCHMITT, M. C., AND C. J. HOPKINS. 1993. "Metacognitive Theory Applied: Strategic Reading Instruction in the Current Generation of Basal Readers." *Reading Research and Instruction* 32 (3): 13–24.

SHANAHAN, T., M. L. KAMIL, AND A. W. TOBIN. 1982. "Cloze as a Measure of Intersentential Comprehension." *Reading Research Quarterly* 17: 229–55.

SMAGORINSKY, P., T. McCANN, AND S. KERN. 1987. *Explorations: Introductory Activities for Literature and Composition, 7–12.* Urbana, IL: National Council of Teachers of English.

STOCKTON, F. R. 1884. *The Lady or the Tiger? And Other Stories.* New York: Charles Scribner and Sons.

TAYLOR, W. 1953. "Cloze Procedure: A New Tool for Measuring Readability." *Journalism Quarterly* 30: 415–33.

TIERNEY, R. J., J. READANCE, AND E. DISHNER. 1995. *Reading Strategies and Practices: A Compendium.* 4th ed. Boston: Allyn and Bacon.

WIGGINS, G., AND J. McTIGHE. 2005. *Understanding by Design.* 2d ed. Alexandria, VA: Association for Supervision and Curriculum Development.

■ Chapter 4

Atkinson, R. K., R. Catrambone, and M. M. Merrill. 2003. "Aiding Transfer in Statistics: Examining the Use of Conceptually Oriented Equations and Elaborations During Subgoal Learning." *Journal of Educational Psychology* 95: 762–73.

Bissinger, H. G. 2000. *Friday Night Lights: A Town, a Team, and a Dream*. New York: De Capo.

Bradford, S. 1869/2006. *Harriet Tubman: The Moses of Her People*. Bedford, MA: Applewood.

Bush, J. n.d. "A Free Conversation with Peter Elbow." *Critique Magazine: On Writing II*. Retrieved June 28, 2008, from www.etext.org/Zines/Critique /writing/elbow.html.

Carr, E., and D. Ogle. 1987. "K-W-L Plus: A Strategy for Comprehension and Summarization." *Journal of Reading* 30: 626–31.

Clinton, C. 2005. *Harriet Tubman: The Road to Freedom*. New York: Back Bay.

Deuker, C. 2007. *Gym Candy*. New York: Houghton Mifflin.

Duncan, D., and E. Mazur. 2005. *Clickers in the Classroom: How to Enhance Science Teaching Using Classroom Response Systems*. New York: Addison-Wesley Professional.

Dutro, S. 2005. "Questions Teachers Are Asking About Courses of Study for Secondary English Language Learners." *The California Reader* 39 (1): 45–58.

Fay, L. 1965. "Reading and Study Skills: Math and Science." In *Reading and Inquiry*, ed. J. A. Figurel, 92–94. Newark, DE: International Reading Association.

Fisher, D., and N. Frey. 2007. *Checking for Understanding: Formative Assessment Techniques for Your Classroom*. Alexandria, VA: Association for Supervision and Curriculum Development.

———. 2008. *Improving Adolescent Literacy: Content Area Strategies at Work*. Upper Saddle River, NJ: Pearson Merrill Prentice Hall.

Frey, N., D. Fisher, and A. Berkin. 2008. *Good Habits, Great Readers: Building the Literacy Community*. Upper Saddle River, NJ: Pearson Merrill Prentice Hall.

Gere, A. R., L. Christenbery, and K. Sassi. 2005. *Writing on Demand: Best Practices and Strategies for Success*. Portsmouth, NH: Heinemann.

GRAFF, G., AND C. BIRKENSTEIN. 2006. *They Say / I Say: The Moves That Matter in Academic Writing*. New York: W. W. Norton.

HUNTER, M. 1976. *Improved Instruction*. Thousand Oaks, CA: Corwin.

KOMAN. K. 1995. "Newton, One-on-One." *The Harvard Journal* (Summer). Retrieved June 30, 2008, from www.columbia.edu/cu/gsapp/BT /RESEARCH/mazur.html.

KRULL, K. 2000. *Lives of Extraordinary Women: Rulers, Rebels (and What the Neighbors Thought)*. San Diego: Harcourt.

LEWIS, M., AND D. WRAY. 1995. *Developing Children's Non-fiction Writing*. New York: Scholastic.

LYON, G. E. 1999. "Where I'm From." *Where I'm From, Where Poems Come From*. Spring, TX: Absey.

MOORE, D., D. ALVERMANN, AND K. HINCHMAN. 2000. *Struggling Adolescent Readers: A Collection of Teaching Strategies*. Newark, DE. International Reading Association.

McGINLEY, W. J., AND P. R. DENNER. 1987. "Story Impressions: A Prereading/ Writing Activity." *Journal of Reading* 31: 248–53.

OGLE, D. 1986. "K-W-L: A Teaching Model That Develops Active Reading of Expository Text." *The Reading Teacher* 39: 564–70.

OKITA, D. 1983. *Breaking Silence: An Anthology of Contemporary Asian American Poets*. Greenfield Center, NY: Greenfield Review.

PARIS, S., D. R. CROSS, AND M. Y. LIPSON. 1984. "Informed Strategies for Learning: A Program to Improve Children's Reading Awareness and Comprehension." *Journal of Educational Psychology* 76: 1239–52.

PICHERT, J. W., AND R. C. ANDERSON. 1977. "Taking Different Perspectives on a Story." *Journal of Educational Psychology* 69: 309–15.

REID, J., P. FORRESTAL, AND J. COOK. 1989. *Small Group Learning in the Classroom*. Portsmouth, NH: Heinemann.

ROBINSON, F. P. 1961. *Effective Study*. Rev. ed. New York: Harper and Row.

ROWLANDS, K. D. 2007. "Check It Out! Using Checklists to Support Student Learning." *English Journal* 96: 61–66.

SCHACTER, D. L. 1999. "The Seven Sins of Memory: Insights from Psychology and Cognitive Neuroscience." *American Psychologist* 54 (3): 182–203.

SCHMUCK, R. A., AND P. A. RUNKEL. 1985. *Handbook of Organizational Development in Schools*. 3d ed. Palo Alto, CA: Mayfield.

STRICKLAND, K., AND J. STRICKLAND. 2000. *Making Assessment Elementary*. Portsmouth, NH: Heinemann.

SZABO, S. 2006. "KWHHL: A Student-Driven Evolution of the K-W-L." *American Secondary Education* 34 (3): 57–67.

TOULMIN, S. 1958. *The Uses of Argument*. New York: Cambridge University Press.

VIORST, J. 1981. *If I Were in Charge of the World and Other Worries: Poems for Children and Their Parents*. New York: Atheneum.

WAGNER, J. F. 2003. "Transfer in Pieces." *Cognition and Instruction* 24: 1–71.

WHITE, K. R. 1974. "T-groups Revisited: Self-Concept Change and the 'Fish-Bowling' Technique." *Small Group Behavior* 5: 473–85.

■ Chapter 5

ALFASSI, M. 2004. "Reading to Learn: Effects of Combined Strategy Instruction on High School Students." *Journal of Educational Research* 97 (4): 171–84.

ALLEN, G. L., C. R. M. COWAN, AND H. POWER. 2006. "Acquiring Information from Simple Weather Maps: Influences of Domain-Specific Knowledge and General Spatial Abilities." *Learning and Individual Differences* 16: 337–49.

ALVERMANN, D. E. 2001. *Effective Literacy Instruction for Adolescents*. Oak Creek, WI: National Reading Conference. Retrieved June 30, 2008, from www.nrconline.org/publications/alverwhite2.pdf.

ANDERSON, R. C. 1977. "The Notion of Schemata and the Educational Enterprise." In *Schooling and the Acquisition of Knowledge*, ed. R. C. Anderson, R. J. Spiro, and W. E. Montague, 415–32. Mahwah, NJ: Lawrence Erlbaum.

ATWELL, N. 1998. *In the Middle: New Understandings About Writing, Reading, and Learning*. Portsmouth, NH: Boynton/Cook.

CONNER, S. A. 2007. *Boredom by Day, Death by Night: An Iraq War Journal*. Wheaton, IL: Tripping Light.

CULLINAN, B. E. 1989. *Literature and the Child*. 2d ed. San Diego: Harcourt Brace Jovanovich.

CUNNINGHAM, A. E., AND K. E. STANOVICH. 1997. "Early Reading Acquisition and Its Relation to Reading Experience and Ability Ten Years Later." *Developmental Psychology* 33: 934–45.

DING, H. 2008. "The Use of Cognitive and Social Apprenticeship to Teach a Disciplinary Genre: Initiation of Graduate Students into NIH Grant Writing." *Written Communication* 25 (3): 3–52.

DOCHY, F., M. SEGERS, AND M. M. BUEHL. 1999. "The Relation Between Assessment Practices and Outcomes of Studies: The Case of Research on Prior Knowledge." *Review of Educational Research* 69 (2): 145–86.

DUFFY, G., L. ROEHLER, E. SILVAN, G. RACKLIFFE, C. BOOK, M. MELOTH, L. VAVRUS, R. WESSELMAN, J. PUTNAM, AND D. BASSIRI. 1987. "Effects of Explaining the Reasoning Associated with Using Strategies." *Reading Research Quarterly* 22: 347–68.

DUNCAN, R. M. 1995. "Piaget and Vygotsky Revisited: Dialogue or Assimilation?" *Developmental Review* 15: 458–72.

FARMER, J., D. KNAPP, AND G. M. BENTON. 2006. "The Effects of Primary Sources and Field Trip Experience on the Knowledge Retention of Multicultural Content." *Multicultural Education* 14 (3): 27–31.

FISHER, D. 2004. "Setting the 'Opportunity to Read' Standard: Resuscitating the SSR Program in an Urban High School." *Journal of Adolescent and Adult Literacy* 48: 138–50.

FISHER, D., AND N. FREY. 2008. *Better Learning Through Structured Teaching: A Framework for the Gradual Release of Responsibility*. Alexandria, VA: Association for Supervision and Curriculum Development.

FISHER, D., N. FREY, AND D. LAPP. 2008. "Shared Readings, Modeling Comprehension, Vocabulary, Text Structures, and Text Features for Older Readers." *The Reading Teacher* 61 (7): 548–56.

FISHER, D., AND G. IVEY. 2006. "Evaluating the Interventions for Struggling Adolescent Readers." *Journal of Adolescent and Adult Literacy* 50: 180–89.

FREY, N. 2006. "Reading in the Park." In *Challenging the Classroom Standard Through Museum-Based Education: School in the Park*, ed. I. Pumpian, D. Fisher, and S. Wachowiak, 43–60. Mahwah, NJ: Lawrence Erlbaum.

———. 2007. *The Effective Teacher's Guide: 50 Ways for Engaging Students in Learning*. San Diego: Academic Professional Development.

GOLDENSOHN, L. 2006. *American War Poetry: An Anthology*. New York: Columbia University Press.

GONZALEZ, N., L. C. MOLL, AND C. AMANTI. 2005. *Funds of Knowledge: Theorizing Practices in Households, Communities, and Classrooms*. Mahwah, NJ: Lawrence Erlbaum.

HASTON, W. 2007. "Teacher Modeling as an Effective Teaching Strategy." *Music Educators Journal* 93 (4): 26–30.

HEGARTY, M., P. A. CARPENTER, AND M. A. JUST. 1991. "Diagrams in the Comprehension of Scientific Text." In *Handbook of Reading Research*, vol. II, ed. R. Barr, M. L. Kamil, P. B. Mosenthal, and P. D. Pearson, 641–88. Mahwah, NJ: Lawrence Erlbaum.

HILL, J., AND K. FLYNN. 2006. *Classroom Instruction That Works with English Language Learners*. Alexandria, VA: Association for Supervision and Curriculum Development.

HOWARD, P. H. 2006. *The Owner's Manual for the Brain: Everyday Applications from Mind-Brain Research*. 3d ed. Austin, TX: Bard.

JACOBSON, S., AND E. COLON. 2006. *The 9/11 Commission Report: A Graphic Adaptation*. New York: Hill and Wang.

JOHNSON, P. 1982. "Effects on Reading Comprehension of Building Background Knowledge." *TESOL Quarterly* 16 (4): 503–16.

KIRSCHNER, P. A., J. SWELLER, AND R. E. CLARK. 2006. "Why Minimal Guidance During Instruction Does Not Work: An Analysis of the Failure of Constructivist, Discovery, Problem-Based, Experiential, and Inquiry-Based Teaching." *Educational Psychologist* 41 (2): 75–86.

KISIEL, J. 2006. "Making Field Trips Work: Strategies for Creating an Effective Learning Experience." *The Science Teacher* 73: 46–48.

MARSHALL, N. 1996. "The Students: Who Are They and How Do I Reach Them?" In *Content Area Reading and Learning: Instructional Strategies*, 2d ed., ed. D. Lapp, J. Flood, and N. Farnan, 79–93. Needham Heights, MA: Allyn and Bacon.

MARZANO, R. J. 2004. *Building Background Knowledge for Academic Achievement: Research on What Works in Schools*. Alexandria, VA: Association for Supervision and Curriculum Development.

MAYER, R. E., AND J. K. GALLINI. 1990. "When Is an Illustration Worth Ten Thousand Words?" *Journal of Educational Psychology* 82 (4): 715–26.

METHE, S. A., AND J. M. HINTZE. 2003. "Evaluating Teacher Modeling as a Strategy to Increase Student Reading Behavior." *School Psychology Review* 32 (4): 617–22.

MYERS, W. D. 2008. *Sunrise over Fallujah*. New York: Scholastic.

OPITZ, M. F., AND T. RASINSKI. 1998. *Good-Bye Round Robin Reading: 25 Effective Oral Reading Strategies*. Portsmouth, NH: Heinemann.

PALINCSAR, A. S., AND A. L. BROWN. 1984. "Reciprocal Teaching of Comprehension-Fostering and Comprehension-Monitoring Activities." *Cognition and Instruction* 1 (1): 117–75.

PAYNE, B. K., M. SUMTER, AND I. SUN. 2003. "Bringing the Field into the Criminal Justice Classroom: Field Trips, Ride-Alongs, and Guest Speakers." *Journal of Criminal Justice Education* 14 (2): 327–44.

PEMBERTON, D. 2005. *The Atlas of Ancient Egypt*. New York: Abrams.

PIAGET, J. 1985. *The Equilibration of Cognitive Structures: The Central Problem of Intellectual Development*. Chicago: University of Chicago Press.

PILGREEN, J. L. 2000. *The SSR Handbook: How to Organize and Manage a Sustained Silent Reading Program*. Portsmouth, NH: Heinemann.

PULIDO, D. 2007. "The Relationship Between Text Comprehension and Incidental Vocabulary Acquisition: A Matter of Familiarity?" *Language Learning* 57 (1): 155–99.

PUMPIAN, I., D. FISHER, AND S. WACHOWIAK, EDS. 2006. *Challenging the Classroom Standard Through Museum-Based Education: School in the Park*. Mahwah, NJ: Lawrence Erlbaum.

ROWLING, J. K. 1997. *Harry Potter and the Sorcerer's Stone*. New York: Scholastic.

SCHONBORN, K. J., AND T. R. ANDERSON. 2006. "The Importance of Visual Literacy in the Education of Biochemists." *Biochemistry and Molecular Biology Education* 34 (2): 94–102.

SCHUNK, D. H. 2007. *Learning Theories: An Educational Perspective*. 5th ed. Upper Saddle River, NJ: Merrill Prentice Hall.

STANOVICH, K. E. 1986. "Matthew Effects in Reading: Some Consequences of Individual Differences in the Acquisition of Reading." *Reading Research Quarterly* 21: 360–407.

STRANGMAN, N., AND T. HALL. 2004. *Background Knowledge*. Wakefield, MA: National Center on Accessing the General Curriculum. Retrieved June 30, 2008, from www.cast.org/publications/ncac/ncac_backknowledge.html.

STAUB, S. D., AND A. P. FINLEY. 2007. "Assessing the Impact of Engaging Learning Initiatives on First-Year Students." *Peer Review* 9 (3): 18–22.

TORRANCE, H. 2007. "Assessment as Learning? How the Use of Explicit Learning Objectives, Assessment Criteria and Feedback in Post-secondary Education and Training Can Come to Dominate Learning." *Assessment in Education: Principles, Policy, and Practice* 14 (3): 281–94.

Tukey, J. W. 1990. "Data-Based Graphics: Visual Displays in the Decades to Come." *Statistical Science* 5: 327–29.

VandeWagne, R. 2006. "Deep Modeling and Authentic Teaching: Challenging Students or Challenging Students?" *English Journal* 95 (4): 84–88.

Vaughan, B. K., and N. Henrichon. 2008. *Pride of Baghdad*. New York: Vertigo.

Vekiri, I. 2002. "What Is the Value of Graphical Displays of Learning?" *Educational Psychology Review* 14: 261–312.

White, E. B. 1952. *Charlotte's Web*. New York: Harper and Row.

Winn, W. 1991. "Learning from Maps and Diagrams." *Educational Psychology Review* 3 (3): 211–47.

Wortman, G. B. 1992. "An Invitation to Learning: Guest Speakers in the Classroom." *The Science Teacher* 59 (2): 19–22.

■ Chapter 6

Avi. 1993. *Nothing but the Truth*. New York: HarperTrophy.

———. 2004. *The True Confessions of Charlotte Doyle*. New York: HarperCollins.

Bridges, R. 1999. *Through My Eyes*. New York: Scholastic.

David, Lawrence 2002. *Beetle Boy*. London: Bloomsbury.

Ellis, Deborah. 2001. *The Breadwinner*. Toronto, ON: Groundwood.

Foss, A. 2002. "Peeling the Onion: Teaching Critical Literacy with Students of Privilege." *Language Arts* 79: 393–403.

Gilligan, C. 2006. "'Mommy, I Know You.' A Feminist Scholar Explains How the Study of Girls Can Teach Us About Boys." *Newsweek* 147 (5): 53.

Kafka, F. 1915/2006. *The Metamorphosis*. West Valley, UT: Waking Lion.

Lee, H. 1960/2002. *To Kill a Mockingbird*. New York: Harper Perennial.

Levine, P., and M. H. Lopez. 2004. *Themes Emphasized in Social Studies and Civics Classes: New Evidence*. College Park, MD: Center for Information and Research on Civic Learning and Engagement. Retrieved April 22, 2007, from www.civicyouth.org/PopUps/FactSheets/FS_Themes_Emphasized_SocStudies_Civics.pdf.

Luke, Allen, and Peter Freebody. 1999. "A Map of Possible Practices: Further Notes on the Four Resources Model." *Practically Primary* 4 (2): 5–8.

McIntosh, P. 1988. "White Privilege: Unpacking the Invisible Knapsack." Retrieved July 5, 2008, from www.nymbp.org/reference/WhitePrivilege.pdf.

McLaughlin, M., and G. L. DeVoogd. 2004. *Critical Literacy: Enhancing Students' Comprehension of Text*. New York: Scholastic.

McLuhan, Marshall. 1962. *The Gutenberg Galaxy: The Making of Typographic Man*. Toronto: University of Toronto Press.

Mosborg, S. 2002. "Speaking of History: How Adolescents Use Their Knowledge of History in Reading the Daily News." *Cognition and Instruction* 20 (3): 323–58.

National Research Council. 2000. *How People Learn: Brain, Mind, Experience, and School*. Committee on Developments in the Science of Learning, J. D. Bransford, A. L. Brown, and R. Cocking (eds.), Commission on Behavioral and Social Sciences and Education. Washington, DC: National Academy Press.

Nelson, P., and H. Scott. 2003. *Left for Dead: A Young Man's Search for Justice for the USS* Indianapolis. New York: Delacorte.

Parker, L., and D. O. Stovall. 2004. "Actions Follow Words: Critical Race Theory Connected to Critical Pedagogy." *Educational Philosophy and Theory* 36 (2): 167–82.

Satrapi, M. 2004. *Persepolis: The Story of a Childhood*. New York: Pantheon.

Sinclair, U. 1994. *I, Candidate for Governor: And How I Got Licked*. Berkley: University of California Press.

Tasmania Department of Education. 2006. *English Learning Area: Critical Literacy*. Retrieved May 31, 2007, from wwwfp.education.tas.gov.au /English/critlit.htm.

van Sluys, K., M. Lewison, and A.S. Flint. 2006. "Researching Critical Literacy: A Critical Study of Analysis of Classroom Discourse." *Journal of Literacy Research* 38: 197–233.

Warren, W. J., D. M. Memory, and K. Bolinger. 2004. "Improving Critical Thinking Skills in a United States History Survey Course: An Activity for Teaching the Vietnam War." *The History Teacher* 37: 193–209.

Wineburg, S. 2001. *Historical Thinking and Other Unnatural Acts: Charting the Future of Teaching the Past*. Philadelphia: Temple University Press.

Wittinger, E. 2007. *Parrotfish*. New York: Simon and Schuster.

▪ Chapter 7

Clark, A. C. 1968. *2001: Space Odyssey*. New York: New American Library.

Coiro, J. 2005. "Making Sense of Online Text." *Educational Leadership* 63 (2): 30–35.

Coiro, J., and E. Dobler. 2007. "Exploring the Online Reading Comprehension Strategies Used by Sixth-Grade Skilled Readers to Search for and Locate Information on the Internet." *Reading Research Quarterly* 42: 214–57.

Dodge, B. 1995. "Webquests: A Technique for Internet-Based Learning." *Distance Educator* 1 (2): 10–13.

Fisher, D., and N. Frey. 2008. "A Positive Test." *Virginia Journal of Education* 102 (3): 15–17.

Langer, J. A. 2001. "Beating the Odds: Teaching Middle and High School Students to Read and Write Well." *American Educational Research Journal* 38: 837–80.

Leu, D. J. Jr. 2008. The New Literacies of Online Reading Comprehension: Preparing All Students for Their Reading Future. Presentation at the San Diego State University Summer Reading Conference, San Diego.

Leu, D. J. Jr., J. Castek, D Hartman, J. Coiro, L. Henry, J. Kulikowich, and S. Lyver. 2005. Evaluating the Development of Scientific Knowledge and New Forms of Reading Comprehension During Online Learning. Research report presented at the North Central Regional Educational Laboratory, Chicago. (Final report presented to the North Central Regional Educational Laboratory/Learning Point Associates). Retrieved July 10, 2008, from www.newliteracies.uconn.edu/ncrel.html.

Leu, D. J. Jr., J. Coiro, J. Castek, D. Hartman, L. Henry, and D. Reinking. 2008. "Research on Instruction and Assessment in the New Literacies of Online Reading Comprehension." In *Comprehension Instruction: Research-Based Best Practices*, ed. C. C. Block and S. Paris, 321–46. New York: Guilford.

Leu, D. J. Jr., D. Reinking, A. Carter, J. Castek, J. Coiro, L. A. Henry, J. Malloy, K. Robbins, A. Rogers, and L. Zawilinski. 2007. *Defining Online Reading Comprehension: Using Think Aloud Verbal Protocols to Refine a Preliminary Model of Internet Reading Comprehension Processes*. Paper presented at the American Educational Research Association, Chicago. Available at http://docs.google.com/Doc?id=dcbjhrtq_10djqrhz.

Pak, M. 2009. "Podcasting: Scaffolding Conceptual Understanding in Writing." *California English* 14 (3): 20–23.

Palincsar, A. S. 1987. "Reciprocal Teaching: Can Student Discussion Boost Comprehension?" *Instructor* 96 (5): 56–58, 60.

SCHWEITZER, N. J. 2008. "Wikipedia and Psychology: Coverage of Concepts and Its Use by Undergraduate Students." *Teaching of Psychology* 35 (2): 81–85.

TABOADA, A., AND J. T. GUTHRIE. 2006. "Contributions of Student Questioning and Prior Knowledge to Construction of Knowledge from Reading Information Text." *Journal of Literacy Research* 38 (1): 1–35.

WATKINS, K. 2008. "Return of the Google Game: More Fun Ideas to Transform Students into Skilled Researchers." *School Library Journal* 54 (5): 46–48.

▪ Chapter 8

BROWN, R. 1991. *Schools of Thought: How the Politics of Literacy Shape Thinking in the Classroom*. San Francisco: Jossey-Bass.

COSTA, A. L., AND B. KALLICK. 2009. *Leading and Learning with Habits of Mind: Sixteen Essential Characteristics for Success*. Alexandria, VA: Association for Supervision and Curriculum Development.

HIRSCH, E. D. 1996. *The Schools We Need and Why We Don't Have Them*. New York: Doubleday.

———. 2002. *What Your Third Grader Needs to Know: Fundamentals of a Good Third-Grade Education*. Rev. ed. New York: Dell.

SQUIRE, J. R. 1988. "Basic Skills Are Not Enough." *Educational Leadership* 45: 76–77.

STERNBERG, R. J. 2008. "The Answer Depends on the Question: A Reply to Eric Jenson." *Phi Delta Kappan* 89: 418–20.

TCHUDI, S. N. 1988. "Slogans Indeed: A Reply to Hirsch." *Educational Leadership* 45: 72–74.

WILLINGHAM, D. 2008. "When and How Neuroscience Applies to Education." *Phi Delta Kappan* 89: 421–23.

Index